STUDY GUIDE
TO BECOME A
NETWORK
ENGINEER

BY

ISAAC DANSO-GYAN

DEDICATION

I dedicate this book to all IT enthusiasts and those who want to
have IT as a professional career in the field of Network
Engineering.

ACKNOWLEDGEMENT

I want to thank all my past students, support staff, friends, and family for their continued support, especially my wife, Phil, and children.

Contents

DEDICATION i

ACKNOWLEDGEMENT ii

INTRODUCTION.. 1

COMPUTER NETWORK.. 2

IP ADDRESSES.. 10

    Types of IP Addresses... 10

DNS (DOMAIN NAME SYSTEM) 14

SUBNET CHART.. 16

REMOTE OFFICE NETWORK SETUP.................................... 20

    Configurations.. 22

    VLAN (Virtual Local Area Network)..................... 26

    Dynamic Host Configuration Protocol (DHCP) 33

ROUTING... 43

ENHANCED INTERIOR GATEWAY ROUTING PROTOCOL
(EIGRP)... 54

    EIGRP automatic & manual summarization 60

OPEN SHORTEST PATH FIRST (OSPF)............................... 63

    OSPF with Multi-Area 68

    OSPF summarization... 71

REDISTRIBUTION OF PROTOCOLS.................................... 72

BORDER GATEWAY PROTOCOL (BGP) 76

WIDE AREA NETWORK (WAN) TECHNOLOGY.................... 83

DATA CENTER DESIGN 97

FIRST HOP REDUNDANCY PROTOCOLS (FHRP) 126

    Hot Standby Routing Protocol (HSRP) 127

    Gateway Load Balancing Protocol (GLBP) 149

ETHER CHANNEL PROTOCOL 156

MULTICAST AND UNICAST NETWORK 160

VIRTUAL SWITCHING SYSTEM 170

VIRTUAL PORTCHANNEL 174

NEXUS VIRTUAL DEVICE CONTEXT (VDC) 183

CLOUD COMPUTING 186

ACCESS CONTROL LIST 195

NAT (NETWORK ADDRESS TRANSLATION) 204

VPN- VIRTUAL PRIVATE NETWORK 208

    GRE VPN – Site-to-Site 217

INTRODUCTION OF FIREWALL IN COMPUTER NETWORK 222

JUNIPER SWITCH MODELS 238

JUNIPER ROUTER MODELS 240

INTRODUCTION

Thank you for purchasing this technical training guide about configuring Cisco routers, switches, firewalls, and Juniper network devices. I firmly believe you have made the right step towards your career in network engineering, which is a rewarding and in-demand IT career path focused on designing, implementing, and managing computer networks.

Network engineers ensure that organizations have secure, efficient, and reliable network infrastructure to support their operations. The field offers diverse opportunities for specialization, high salary potential, and the ability to work remotely. Cisco has a large market share in the hardware market, so learning to configure and implement the appliance guarantees a successful career in this field.

This book is the result of my working experience over the years in the industry and summarizes the most important features and most frequent configuration scenarios that a network engineer will encounter in real-world networks. I have summarized the vast volume in a handy, directly applicable book that will get you on track right away. You can use this book together with other resource documentation or a reference guide for most of the common commands in Cisco networking.

For any questions that you may have about the information in this book or a lab access to practice along please contact me at training@networkprofessional.net

Wishing you well in your new endeavor.

COMPUTER NETWORK

A computer network is a system of interconnected devices that enables the sharing of resources and information. Nodes in a network are connected with each other using either cable or wireless media.

Nodes can include hosts such as personal computers, phones, printers, cameras, and servers, as well as networking hardware. Two such devices can be said to be networked together when one device is able to exchange information with the other device.

TYPES OF NETWORKS

LANs Local Area Network linking a limited area such as a home, office, or a small group of buildings

WANs Wide Area Network, which links nationally or internationally

SAN Storage Area Network

GAN Global Area Networks, combining all of the above with satellite mobile communication technologies

VoIP Voice over Internet Protocol Network

WLAN Wireless Local Area Network

INTERNET

It is a global network of millions of private, public, and organizational networks. It carries a massive range of informational resources and data in the form of HTTP (Hypertext Markup language) documents and applications through the World Wide Web (WWW).

INTRANET

An intranet is an exclusive network that can be accessed only by a specific group of people and no one else. Many corporations, government agencies, and universities have their own intranets.

EXTRANET

An extranet is a controlled private network that allows access to partners, vendors, and suppliers or an authorized set of customers. Extranets are typically constructed using the Internet with security features that restrict access to authorized individuals and digital entities.

LAN (LOCAL AREA NETWORK)

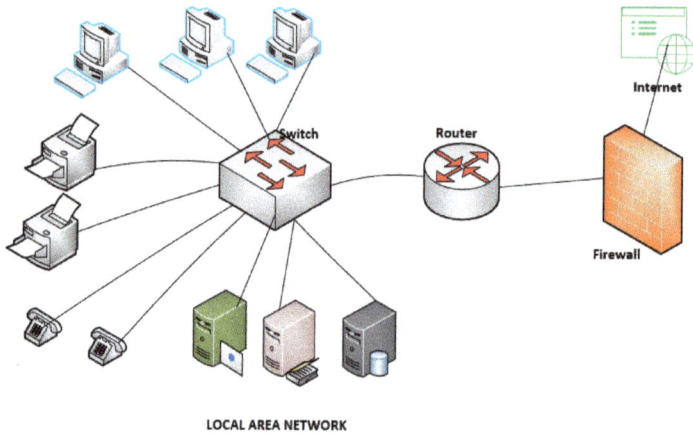

LOCAL AREA NETWORK

WAN (WIDE AREA NETWORK)

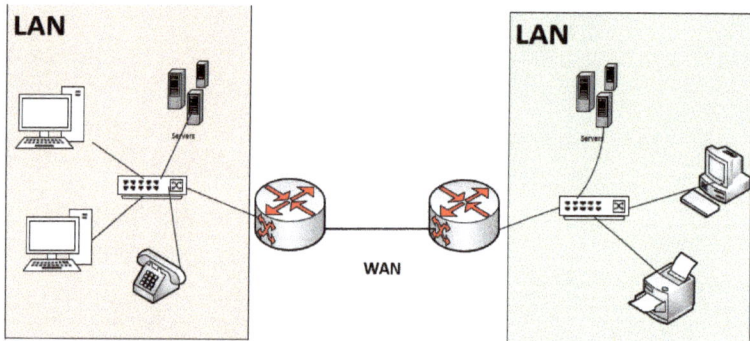

Interview Questions

IQ: Explain what you know about intranet and extranet.

IQ: What is the difference between LAN and WAN?

NETWORK DEVICES

The common network devices used in real life to help communication are routers, switches, firewalls, and access points.

Routers

The router is a network device that connects two or more network segments. The router is used to transfer information from the source to the destination.

Routers send the information in terms of data packets. When these data packets are forwarded from one router to another router, the router reads the network address in the packets and identifies the destination network.

Switches

A switch is a device that is used to connect many devices together on a computer network.

CISCO ROUTER FRONT AND BACK VIEW

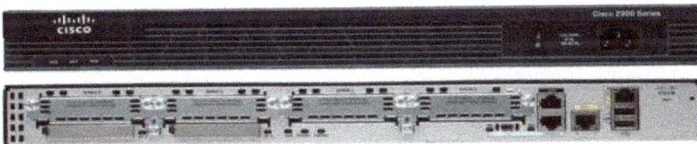

CISCO SWITCH FRONT AND BACK VIEW

ROUTER AND SWITCH FEATURES

	Router	Switch
Function	A router is a networking device that is used to connect two or more networks.	A network switch is a computer networking device that is used to connect many devices together on a computer network.
Ports	2/4/5/8 ports	24/48 ports
Used in LAN, WAN	LAN, WAN	LAN
Table	Store the IP address in the routing table and maintain the address on its own	Store Mac addresses in the CAM table.
Broadcast Domain	Every port has its own broadcast domain	Switch has one broadcast domain [unless VLAN is implemented]
Address used for Data Transmission	Uses IP address	Uses MAC address

Access Point

Access points are used for extending the wireless coverage of an existing network and for increasing the number of users that can connect to it. Wireless connectivity is typically the only available option for access points, establishing links with end devices using Wi-Fi.

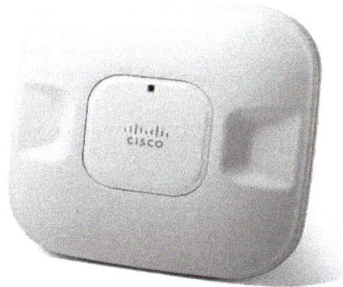

Firewall

A firewall is a network security system that is used to protect computer networks from unauthorized access. It prevents malicious access from outside the computer network. A firewall can also be built to grant limited access to outside users.

The firewall consists of a hardware device, a software program, or a combined configuration of both. All the messages that route through the firewall are examined by specific security criteria, and the messages that meet the criteria are successfully traversed through the network, or else those messages are blocked.

Firewalls can be installed just like any other computer software, and later can be customized as per the need, and have some control over the access and security features.

"Windows Firewall" is an inbuilt Microsoft Windows application that comes along with the operating system. This "Windows Firewall" also helps to prevent viruses, worms, etc.

Firewall virus protection observes traffic in the network, thereby inhibiting malicious data from entering the network, hence thwarting viruses. However, the virus can enter your computer through a spam link, download, or from a flash drive. Moreover, once it bypasses the firewall protection, the antivirus role comes in handy.

Even though the firewall halts the malware and viruses from entering the system, it cannot delete the cyber threat that is infecting the system.

Antivirus

Antivirus software is a cybersecurity mechanism that many PCs and offices use. Its primary function is to scan, spot, and inhibit any apprehensive or distrustful files and software from getting into the system.

Below is a comparison chart. It can help you identify the differences between the two mechanisms.

Basis For Comparison	Firewall	Antivirus
Implemented in	Both Hardware and Software	Software only
Operations Performed	Monitoring and Filtering (Specifically IP Filtering)	Scanning of infected files and software
Deals with	External Threats	Internal as well as external threats
Inspection of Attack is based on	Incoming Packets	Malicious software residing on a computer
Counter Attacks	IP spoofing and routing attacks	No counter attacks are possible once a malware has removed

IP ADDRESSES

Every machine on a network has a unique identifier. Just as you would address a letter to send in the mail, computers use a unique identifier to send data to specific computers on a network. Most networks today, including all computers on the Internet, use the TCP/IP protocol as the standard for how to communicate on the network. In the TCP/IP protocol, the unique identifier for a computer is called its IP address.

All **IP ADDRESSES** are divided into two portions: the **NETWORK ADDRESS** and the **HOST ADDRESS**. E.g. 192.168.3.1

[**192.168.3**] – Network address and **1** - Host address

There are two standards for IP addresses: IP Version 4 (IPv4) and IP Version 6 (IPv6).

Types of IP Addresses

Public (External) IP Addresses

A public (or *external*) IP address is the one that your ISP *(Internet Service Provider)* provides to identify your home network to the outside world. It is an IP address that is unique throughout the entire Internet.

Private Addresses

When several computers or devices are connected to each other, either with cables or wirelessly, they can make up a private network. Each device within this network is assigned a different IP address in order to exchange files and share resources within the network.

CLASSES OF IP ADDRESSES

Class	IP Address Range	Number of Addresses	Subnet Mask
A	10.0.0.0 - 10.255.255.255	16,777,216	255.0.0.0
B	172.16.0.0 - 172.31.255.255	1,048,576	255.255.0.0
C	192.168.0.0 - 192.168.255.255	65,536	255.255.255.0
D	224.0.0.0 - 239.255.255.255	N/A	N/A
E	240.0.0.0 - 255.255.255.255	N/A	N/A

APIPA – Automatic Private IP Addressing

Windows operating systems. With APIPA, DHCP clients can automatically self-configure an IP address and subnet mask when a DHCP server isn't available.

The IP address range is **169.254.0.1** through **169.254.255.254**.

Loopback Address

A loopback address is a special IP number (**127.0.0.1**) that is designated for the software loopback interface of a machine. The loopback interface has no hardware associated with it, and it is not physically connected to a network.

The loopback interface allows IT professionals to test IP software without worrying about broken or corrupted drivers or hardware.

How to find out your IP address

If you are using Windows, start the Command Prompt (Start – Programs – Accessories – Command Prompt). Enter the *IPconfig* command. You should see a field called **IP address:**

```
Command Prompt                                                    _| |O| x|
C:\Users\user>ipconfig

Windows IP Configuration

Ethernet adapter Local Area Connection:

    Connection-specific DNS Suffix  . : localdomain
    Link-local IPv6 Address . . . . . : fe80::b82d:1c2b:ed4d:b89d%11
    IPv4 Address. . . . . . . . . . . : 10.10.100.131
    Subnet Mask . . . . . . . . . . . : 255.255.255.0
    Default Gateway . . . . . . . . . :

Tunnel adapter isatap.localdomain:

    Media State . . . . . . . . . . . : Media disconnected
    Connection-specific DNS Suffix  . : localdomain

C:\Users\user>_
```

MAC Address

Every network card manufacturer gets a universally unique 3-byte code called the **Organizationally Unique Identifier (OUI)**. Manufacturers agree to give all NICs a MAC address that begins with the assigned OUI. The manufacturer then assigns a unique value for the last 3 bytes, which ensures that every MAC address is globally unique.

MAC addresses are usually written in the form of 12 hexadecimal digits. For example, consider the following MAC address:

D8-D3-85-EB-12-E3

How to find out your own MAC address and IP address on a PC?

If you are using Windows, start the Command Prompt (Start – Programs – Accessories – Command Prompt). Type the *IPconfig/all* command, and you should see a field called Physical Address under the Ethernet adapter settings:

```
Command Prompt

C:\Users\user>ipconfig /all

Windows IP Configuration

   Host Name . . . . . . . . . . . . : WIN-7NHASUKCI7D
   Primary Dns Suffix  . . . . . . . :
   Node Type . . . . . . . . . . . . : Hybrid
   IP Routing Enabled. . . . . . . . : No
   WINS Proxy Enabled. . . . . . . . : No
   DNS Suffix Search List. . . . . . : localdomain

Ethernet adapter Local Area Connection:

   Connection-specific DNS Suffix  . : localdomain
   Description . . . . . . . . . . . : Intel(R) PRO/1000 MT Network Connection
   Physical Address. . . . . . . . . : 00-0C-29-6C-F3-E5
   DHCP Enabled. . . . . . . . . . . : Yes
   Autoconfiguration Enabled . . . . : Yes
   Link-local IPv6 Address . . . . . : fe80::b82d:1e2b:ed4d:b89d:11(Preferred)
   IPv4 Address. . . . . . . . . . . : 10.10.100.131(Preferred)
   Subnet Mask . . . . . . . . . . . : 255.255.255.0
   Lease Obtained. . . . . . . . . . : Monday, March 25, 2013 2:34:36 PM
   Lease Expires . . . . . . . . . . : Monday, March 25, 2013 3:04:36 PM
   Default Gateway . . . . . . . . . : 10.10.100.254
   DHCP Server . . . . . . . . . . . : 10.10.100.254
   DHCPv6 IAID . . . . . . . . . . . : 234884137
   DHCPv6 Client DUID. . . . . . . . : 00-01-00-01-18-C6-CD-56-00-0C-29-6C-F3-E5

   DNS Servers . . . . . . . . . . . : 10.10.100.1
   NetBIOS over Tcpip. . . . . . . . : Enabled

Tunnel adapter isatap.localdomain:

   Media State . . . . . . . . . . . : Media disconnected
   Connection-specific DNS Suffix  . : localdomain
   Description . . . . . . . . . . . : Microsoft ISATAP Adapter
   Physical Address. . . . . . . . . : 00-00-00-00-00-00-00-E0
   DHCP Enabled. . . . . . . . . . . : No
   Autoconfiguration Enabled . . . . : Yes

C:\Users\user>
```

Interview Questions

IQ: What is the difference between a Private and a Public IP address?

IQ: Give examples of Private and Public IP addresses.

IQ: What are APIPA and Loopback Addresses?

IQ: What is the difference between a physical address and a logical address?

Answer:

Physical Address: It's called a MAC Address (48-bit).

Logical Address: It's called an IP Address (IPv4 -32 bit & IPv6 - 128 bit).

DNS (DOMAIN NAME SYSTEM)

DNS (Domain Name System) is a network protocol that we use to find the IP addresses of hostnames. Computers use IP addresses, but for us humans, it's more convenient to use domain names and hostnames instead of IP addresses. If you want, you could visit networkprofession.net by going directly to the IP address 95.85.36.216, but typing in the domain name networkprofessional.net is probably easier.

There are thousands of DNS servers, but none of them has a complete database with all hostnames/domain names and IP addresses. A DNS server might have information for certain domains but might have to query other DNS servers if it doesn't have an answer.

There are 13 root name servers that have information for the generic top-level domains like com, net, org, biz, edu, or country-specific domains like UK, NL, DE, BE, AU, CA, and such.

The figure below explains the concept:

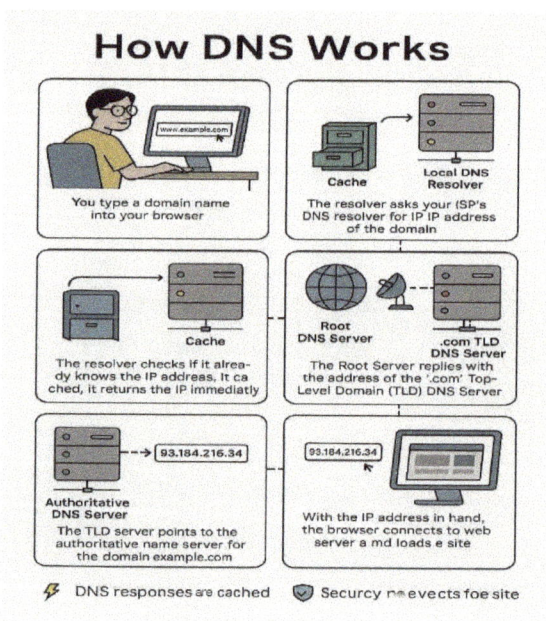

How DNS Works

You type a domain name into your browser

The resolver asks your ISP's DNS resolver for IP IP address of the domain

Cache / **Local DNS Resolver**

The resolver checks if it already knows the IP address. It cached, it returns the IP immediatly

Cache

The Root Server replies with the address of the '.com' Top-Level Domain (TLD) DNS Server

Root DNS Server / **.com TLD DNS Server**

The TLD server points to the authoritative name server for the domain example.com

Authoritative DNS Server — 93.184.216.34

With the IP address in hand, the browser connects to web server a md loads e site

93.184.216.34

⚡ DNS responses are cached   🛡 Securcy re evects foe site

NOTE:

DNS uses a well-known UDP port 53.

To verify if DNS is working = type nslookup under the command prompt.

```
Select Command Prompt - nslookup

Microsoft Windows [Version 10.0.17763.379]
(c) 2018 Microsoft Corporation. All rights reserved.

C:\Users\Initial User>nslookup
Default Server:  www.routerlogin.com
Address:  192.168.1.1
```

Interview Question

IQ: Explain what you know about DNS.

SUBNET CHART

CIDR	Subnet Mask	Wildcard Mask	Total IPs	Usable IPs
/32	255.255.255.255	0.0.0.0	1	1
/31	255.255.255.254	0.0.0.1	2	0
/30	255.255.255.252	0.0.0.3	4	2
/29	255.255.255.248	0.0.0.7	8	6
/28	255.255.255.240	0.0.0.15	16	14
/27	255.255.255.224	0.0.0.31	32	30
/26	255.255.255.192	0.0.0.63	64	62
/25	255.255.255.128	0.0.0.127	128	126
/24	255.255.255.0	0.0.0.255	256	254
/23	255.255.254.0	0.0.1.255	512	510
/22	255.255.252.0	0.0.3.255	1024	1022
/21	255.255.248.0	0.0.7.255	2048	2046
/20	255.255.240.0	0.0.15.255	4096	4094
/19	255.255.224.0	0.0.31.255	8192	8190

www.networkprofessional.net   training@networkprofessional.net   774-253-6228 1 508-859-0440

CIDR	Subnet Mask	Wildcard Mask	Total IPs	Usable IPs
/18	255.255.192.0	0.0.63.255	16,384	16,382
/17	255.255.128.0	0.0.127.255	32,768	32,766
/16	255.255.0.0	0.0.255.255	65,536	65,534
/15	255.254.0.0	0.1.255.255	131,072	131,070
/14	255.252.0.0	0.3.255.255	262,144	262,142
/13	255.248.0.0	0.7.255.255	524,288	524,286
/12	255.240.0.0	0.15.255.255	1,048,576	1,048,574
/11	255.224.0.0	0.31.255.255	2,097,152	2,097,150
/10	255.192.0.0	0.63.255.255	4,194,304	4,194,302
/9	255.128.0.0	0.127.255.255	8,388,608	8,388,606
/8	255.0.0.0	0.255.255.255	16,777,216	16,777,214
/7	254.0.0.0	1.255.255.255	33,554,432	33,554,430
/6	252.0.0.0	3.255.255.255	67,108,864	67,108,862
/5	248.0.0.0	7.255.255.255	134,217,728	134,217,726

CIDR	Subnet Mask	Wildcard Mask	Total IPs	Usable IPs
/4	240.0.0.0	15.255.255.255	268,435,456	268,435,454
/3	224.0.0.0	31.255.255.255	536,870,912	536,870,910
/2	192.0.0.0	63.255.255.255	1,073,741,824	1,073,741,822
/1	128.0.0.0	127.255.255.255	2,147,483,648	2,147,483,646
/0	0.0.0.0	255.255.255.255	4,294,967,296	4,294,967,294

HOW TO ACCESS THE CISCO IOS CLI

Before we can enter any commands, we need access to the CLI. There are three options:

- Console
- Telnet
- SSH

The console is a physical port on the switch that allows access to the CLI. We typically use this the first time we configure the switch. Telnet and SSH are both options for remote access with the help of terminal software, e.g., Putty, SecureCRT, etc.

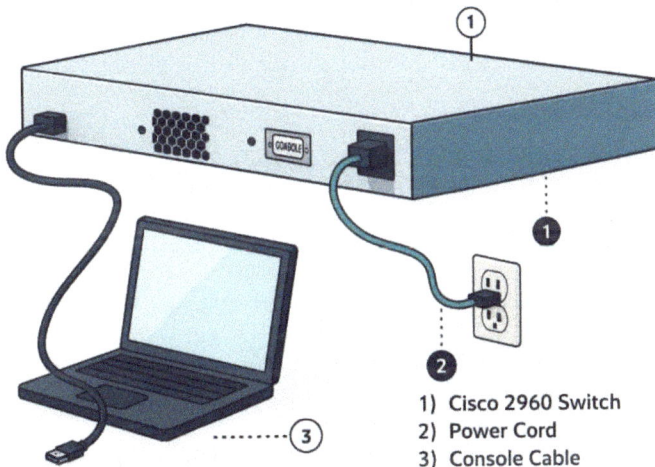

1) Cisco 2960 Switch
2) Power Cord
3) Console Cable

Operating Systems for Cisco Devices

- Internetwork Operating System (IOS)
- CatOS—Catalyst Switch Operating System
- NX-OS—Nexus Operating System

REMOTE OFFICE NETWORK SETUP

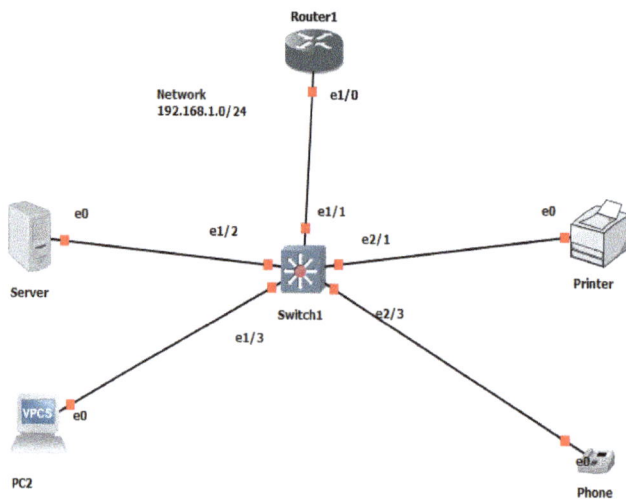

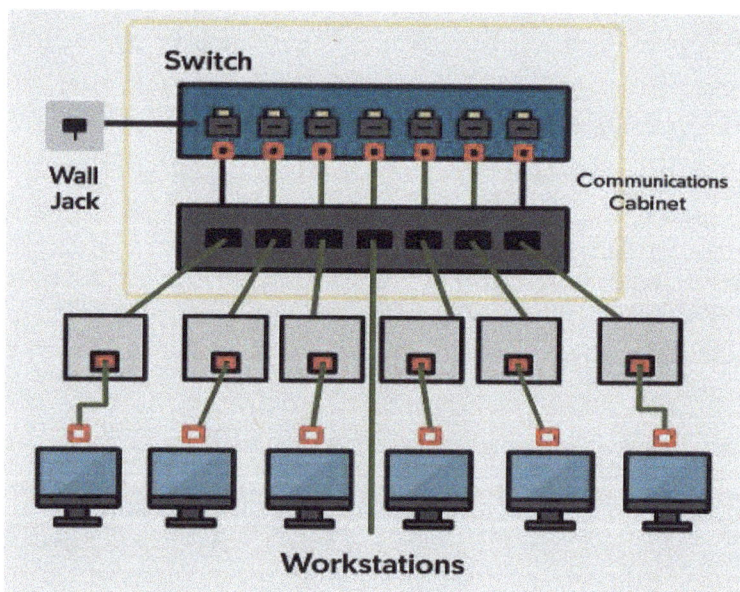

Router1

Network
192.168.1.0/24

e1/0

e1/1

e0   e0

e1/2   e2/1

Server   **Switch1**   **Printer**

e2/3

e1/3

VPCS
e0

PC2

e0

Phone

Switch

Wall
Jack

Communications
Cabinet

Workstations

HOW IT IS WIRED IN REAL LIFE

Data Closet

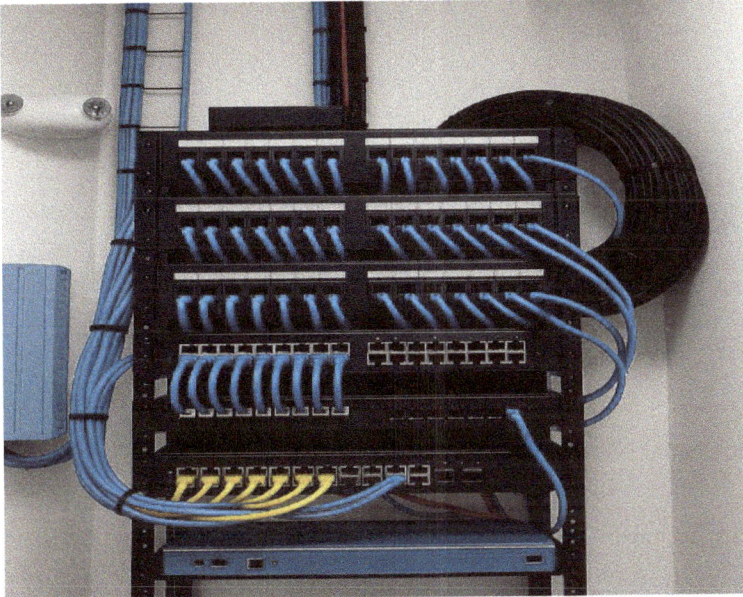

Office Cable Setup

WALL JACK

COMPUTER

Basic Setup LAB 1

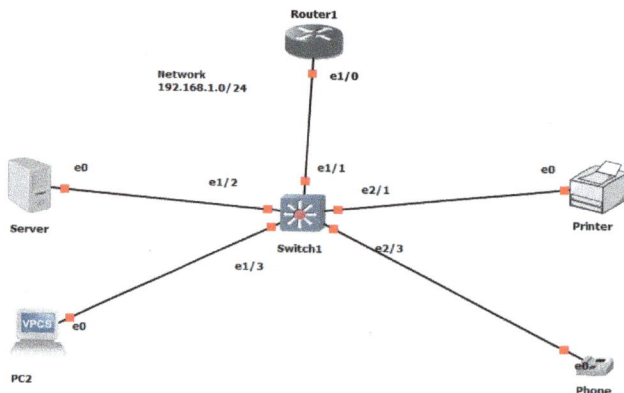

Configurations

1. Configure your router and switch with the following basic information.

Cisco Operational Mode

R1>User Mode

R1>enable	Enter Privilege mode
R1#	Privilege mode
R# conf t	Enter Configuration mode
R(config)#	Global Config mode

Global Configurations

RI(config)#hostname Internet_Router	Changes hostname
Internet_Router (config)#no IP domain-lookup	Disables DNS lookup
Internet_Router(config)#enable secret NPTC	Assigns NPTC as the secret password.

| Internet_Router(config)#service password-encryption | Encrypts any password stored in clear text. |

Line Con 0 Configurations

| Internet_Router(config)#lin con 0 | Enters console port configurations |

| Internet_Router(config-lin)#password c | Sets console password to c |

| Internet_Router(config-lin)#logging synchronous | Synchronize messages to keep what you have typed on the screen. |

| Internet_Router(config-lin)#exec-timeout 45 20 | Sets timeout to 45 minutes and 20 secs |

Line vty Configuration

| Internet_Router(config)#lin vty 0 4 | Establishes 5 possible telnet sessions. |

| Internet_Router(config-lin)#pass v | Sets v as telnet password. |

| Internet_Router(config-line)#logg syn | Synchronize messages to keep what you have typed on a screen |

| Internet_Router(config-line)#exec-timeout 0 0 | Disables timeout |

How to end and save your config

| Internet_Router (config-line)#exit or end | Return to Privilege mode |

| Internet_Router# wr or copy run start | Save Config. |

| Internet_Router# disable | Return user mode |

Internet_Router > enable   Return to Privilege mode.

IQ: What is the basic configuration for network devices, e.g., routers and switches?

Verify your configuration by show run.

Building configuration...

Current configuration: 1692 bytes

Version 12.4

service timestamps debug date time msec

service timestamps log date time msec

service password-encryption

hostname Router

boot-start-marker

boot-end-marker

enable secret 5 1wedi$gX01LUMyMa64txT3oUBUQ.

noaaa new-model

noIPicmp rate-limit unreachable

IPcef

no IP domain lookup

IPtcpsynwait-time 5

no IP http secure-server

line con 0

exec-timeout 45 20

privilege level 15

password 7 0508

logging synchronous

linevty 0 4

exec-timeout 0 0

password 7 051D

logging synchronous

2. **Assign the IP address to the Router and describe the port and the network.**

Router (Config) #**int e1 /0**

Description Switch_e1 /1

#No shut

#Int e1 /0.10

#Description Accounts

#Encapsulation dot1 Q 10

IP address 192.168.1.1 255.255.255.0

Verify your Port configuration

Show run int e1 /0.10

Interface ethernet1 /0.10

Description Accounts

Encapsulation dot1 Q 10

IP address 192.168.1.1 255.255.255.0

Verify your Config: Show IP int Brief

Router# show IP int br

Interface	IP-Address	OK? Method	Status	Protocol
Ethernet1 /0	unassigned	YES TFTP	up	up
Ethernet1 /0.10	192.168.1.1	YES manual	up	up

VLAN (Virtual Local Area Network)

A **VLAN (Virtual Local Area Network)** is a logical grouping of network users and resources connected to defined ports on a switch. By default, all ports on a switch are in the same broadcast domain. A Virtual Local Area Network, Virtual LAN, or VLAN, can be used to divide a single broadcast domain into multiple broadcast domains in a layer 2 switched network.

Default VLAN

The **Default VLAN** is simply the VLAN to which all Access Ports are assigned until they are explicitly placed in another VLAN. In the case of Cisco switches (and most other Vendors), the Default VLAN is usually VLAN 1.

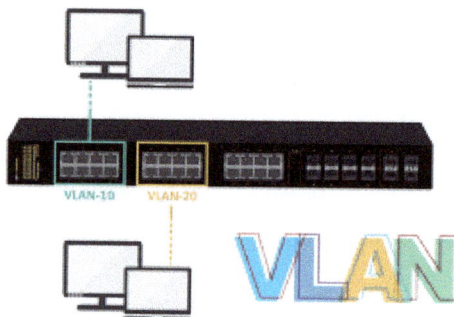

What are the advantages of using VLANs?

- VLANs enable logical grouping of end stations that are physically dispersed on a network.
- Added security by keeping devices in a certain group (or function) in a separate Broadcast domain.
- Higher performance and reduced latency.

3. Configure VLAN 10 on the switch and name it Accounts

Switch (Config) #**VLAN** 10

Name Accounts

Verify your Config: Show VLAN brief.

Switch# show VLAN br

VLAN	Name	Status	Ports
1	default	active	Et0/0, Et0/1, Et0/2, Et0/3
			Et1 /0, Et1 /1, Et1 /2, Et1 /3
			Et2/0, Et2/1, Et2/2, Et2/3
			Et3/0, Et3/1, Et3/2, Et3/3
10	Accounts	active	
1002	fddi-default	act/unsup	
1003	token-ring-default	act/unsup	
1004	fddinet-default	act/unsup	
1005	trnet-default	act/unsup	

4. Configure the switch virtual interface (SVI) on all the switches

Switch Virtual Interface (SVI)

A **Switched Virtual Interface** (SVI) represents a logical layer-3 interface on a switch. There is no physical interface for the VLAN, and the SVI provides the Layer 3 processing for packets from all switch ports associated with the VLAN.

SVI Configuration

Switch (config) # interface VLAN 10

IP address 192.168.1.2 255.255.255.0

no shut

5. Configure a Switch Default Gateway

Switch Default Gateway

The switch should be configured with a default gateway if the switch will be managed remotely from networks not directly connected. A default gateway is a router that hosts use to communicate with other hosts on remote networks.

Switch (config) # IP default-gateway 192.168.1.1

6. **Configure the Trunk Port on the switch connected to the router and describe the port.**

Trunk Port –Transmit the data traffic of multiple VLANs simultaneously. Generally, a Trunk link is configured between the switch to switch or switch to the router.

Switch (Config) # int e1 /1

Description Internet_router_e1 /0

switchport trunk encapsulation dot1 q

switchport mode Trunk

Verify Config: Show int trunk

Port	Mode	Encapsulation	Status	Native VLAN
Et1 /1	on	802.1q	trunking	1

Port	VLANS allowed on trunk
Et1 /1	1-4094

Port	VLANS allowed and active in the management domain
Et1 /1	1,10

Port   VLANS in spanning tree forwarding state and not pruned

7. Configure the access port to all connected PC base on the VLAN

Access port – The access port belongs to and transmits the traffic of only one VLAN at a time. Any data frame received on an access port is simply supposed to belong to the VLAN configured on that port.

Switch (Config)# int e1/2

     # switchport access VLAN 10

     # switch mode Access

     # Spanning-tree portfast

Switch (Config)# int e1/3

     # switchport access VLAN 10

     # switch mode Access

     # Spanning-tree portfast

Switch (Config)# int e2/1

     # switchport access VLAN 10

     # switch mode Access

     # Spanning-tree portfast

Switch (Config)# int e2/3

     # switchport access VLAN 10

     # switch mode Access

     # Spanning-tree portfast

Configuration in a range format

Int range e1 /2 – 3

        # switchport access VLAN 10

        # switch mode Access

        # Spanning-tree portfast

Verify Config: Show int status

Switch# show int status

Port	Name	Status	VLAN	Duplex	Speed Type
Et1 /	Internet_ router_e 1 /0	connected	trunk	full	100 10/100Ba seTX
Et1 /2		connected	10	full	100 10/100Ba seTX
Et1 /3		connected	10	full	100 10/100Ba seTX
Et2/1		connected	10	full	100 10/100Ba seTX
Et2/3		connected	10	full	100 10/100Ba seTX

8. Assign a Static IP address to the PC

PC1>IP 192.168.1.3   255.255.255.0   192.168.1.1

  PC2>IP 192.168.1.4   255.255.255.0   192.168.1.1

Verify Config: Show IP

Interview Question for Practice

IQ: What is the difference between an access port and a trunk?

IQ: How can you add an interface to a VLAN?

IQ: How do you configure a trunk link?

BASIC SETUP ASSIGNMENT

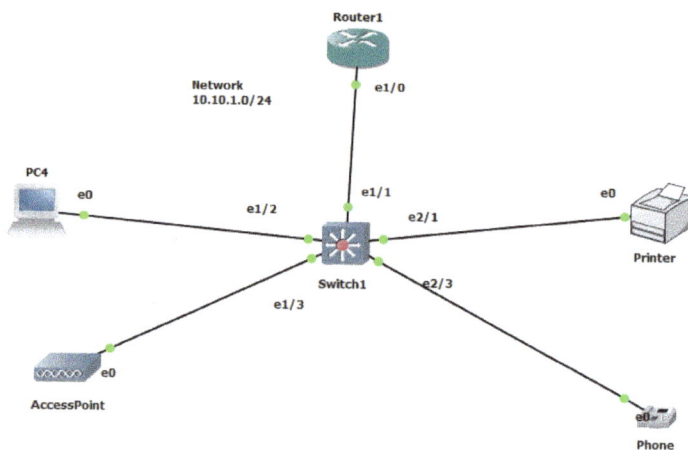

1. Configure your router and switch with basic information.
2. Assign an IP address to the router and describe the port and the network.
3. Configure the hostname of the switch (ESW1) as Data_Switch.
4. Configure the Trunk Port on the switch connected to the router and describe the port.
5. Configure the Trunk Port on the switch connected to the router and describe the port.
6. Configure the Access port to all connected devices base on the VLAN.
7. Configure the switch virtual interface (SVI) on the switch.
8. Configure a Switch Default Gateway.
9. Assign a Static IP address to the PC.

Dynamic Host Configuration Protocol (DHCP)

DHCP is a network protocol that is used to assign various network parameters to a device. This greatly simplifies the administration of a network since there is no need to assign static network parameters for each device.

IP addresses can be configured **statically** or **dynamically**. Normally, we configure static IP addresses on network devices like routers, switches, firewalls, and servers while we dynamically assign IP addresses to computers, laptops, tablets, smartphones, etc.

The DHCP server maintains a pool of available IP addresses and assigns one of them to the host. A DHCP server can also provide some other parameters, such as:

- subnet mask
- default gateway
- domain name
- DNS server

Cisco routers can be configured as DHCP servers.

DHCP process explained:

The DHCP client goes through the four-step process:

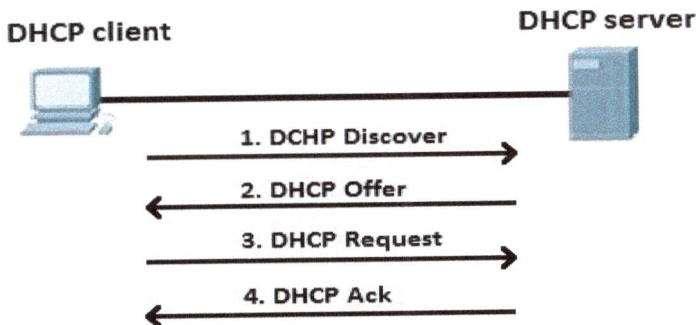

1: A DHCP client sends a broadcast packet (**DHCP Discover**) to discover DHCP servers on the LAN segment.

2: The DHCP servers receive the DHCP Discover packet and respond with **DHCP Offer** packets, offering IP addressing information.

3: If the client receives the DHCP Offer packets from multiple DHCP servers, the first DHCP Offer packet is accepted. The client responds by broadcasting a **DHCP Request** packet, requesting the network parameters from the server that responded first.

4: The DHCP server approves the lease with a **DHCP Acknowledgement** packet. The packet includes the lease duration and other configuration information.

NOTE

DHCP uses a well-known UDP port number 67 for the DHCP server and the UDP port number 68 for the client.

DHCP LAB TASK # 2

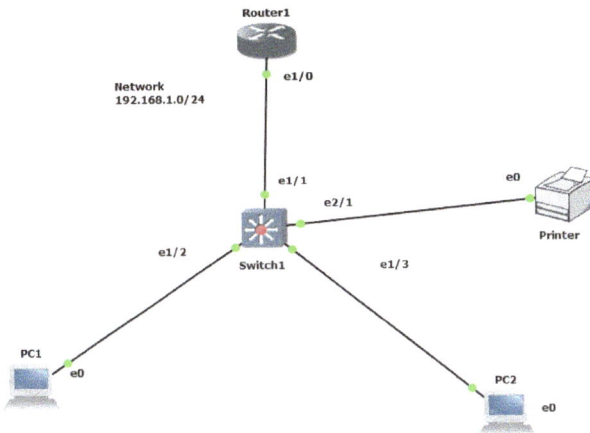

Global Configuration

1. Configure the hostname base on the Network Diagram.
2. Disable the DNS lookup feature.
3. Assign Cisco as the Secret password.
4. Direct the Cisco IOS to encrypt any passwords stored in clear text.

Console Port

1. Configure the console port on all devices to log input synchronously.
2. Set the password to NPTC!
3. Configure the idling timeout to 1 hour and 30 seconds.

VTY Ports

1. Allow 5 concurrent sessions of remote access.
2. Configure the vty ports to log input synchronously.
3. Set the password to VAN.
4. Configure idling timeout to 30 mins and 10 secs.
5. Save config.

Verify config

- Assign the IP address to the router

Verify config

- Configure the router to act as a DHCP Server and reserve 10 IP addresses for static.

Internet_Router (config) #IP DHCP pool Marketing

Network 192.168.1.0 255.255.255.0

default-router 192.168.1.1

Lease 3 0 (interpreted as follows: 3 days, 0 hours and 0 minutes)

IP dhcp excluded-address 192.168.1.1 **192.168.1.10**

Verify config

Show run | begin dhcp

- **Configure the VLAN on the switch and name it as follows**

VLAN 50- Marketing Department

Verify config

- Configure the switch virtual interface (SVI) on the switch
- Configure a Switch Default Gateway
- Configure the Trunk Port based on the topology

Verify config

- Assign VLAN to all the PCs based on the Network topology

Verify config

- Obtain the DHCP address to the PCs and assign a static IP address to the printer.

Verify config

Show Command for DHCP

Show run | begin DHCP

Show IP dhcp binding

LAB OBJECTIVE

- Verify if there is communication between the two PC and the printer.

Interview Questions for Practice

IQ: What is DHCP?

IQ: How does DHCP work?

DHCP LAB TASK#3

Router1
Network
192.168.1.0/24 vlan 100 Accounts
10.10.1.0/24 vlan 200 Engineering

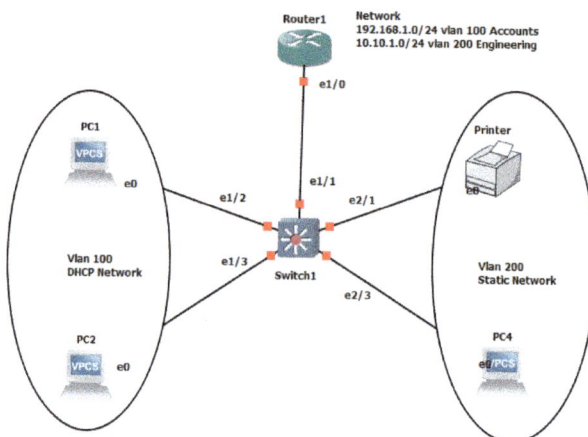

Global Configuration

1. Configure the hostname base on the Network Diagram.
2. Disable the DNS lookup feature.
3. Assign IK@ as the Secret password.
4. Direct the Cisco IOS to encrypt any passwords stored in clear text.

Console Port

5. Configure the console port on all devices to log input synchronously.
6. Set the password to @NPTC.
7. Configure the idling timeout to 1 hour and 50 mins.

VTY Ports

8. Allow 5 concurrent sessions of remote access.
9. Configure the vty ports to log input synchronously.
10. Set password to Pa$$co.
11. Configure idling timeout to 50 mins and 10 secs.
12. Save config.

Verify config

- Assign an IP address to the router and describe the port and network.

Router (Config)#**int e1 /0**

> # Description Switch_e1 /1
>
> #No shut
>
> #Int e1 /0.100
>
> #Description Accounts
>
> #Encapsulation dot1 Q 100
>
> # IP address 192.168.1.1 255.255.255.0

> #Int e1 /0.200
>
> #Description Engineering
>
> #Encapsulation dot1 Q 200
>
> # IP address 10.10.1.1 255.255.255.0

Verify config

- Configure the router to act as a DHCP Server and exclude 20 IP addresses from the Accounts Scope.

Internet_Router(config)# IP DHCP pool Accounts

> # Network 192.168.1.0 255.255.255.0
>
> #default-router 192.168.1.1
>
> # Lease 3 0
>
> # IP dhcp excluded-address 192.168.1.1 192.168.1.20

Verify config

Show run | begin DHCP

- Configure the VLAN 100 and 200 on the switch and name it as follows.

VLAN 100- Accounts Department

VLAN 200 – Engineering Department

Verify config

- Configure the switch virtual interface (SVI) using VLAN 100 on the switch
- Configure a Switch Default Gateway
- Configure the Trunk Port to the port connected to the router and the switch, and describe the port connections.

Verify config

- Assign VLAN to all the PCs and the printer base on the Network topology

Verify config

- Obtain the DHCP address to the PCs and assign a static IP address to the printer and PC 4.

Verify config

DHCP Lab Assignment

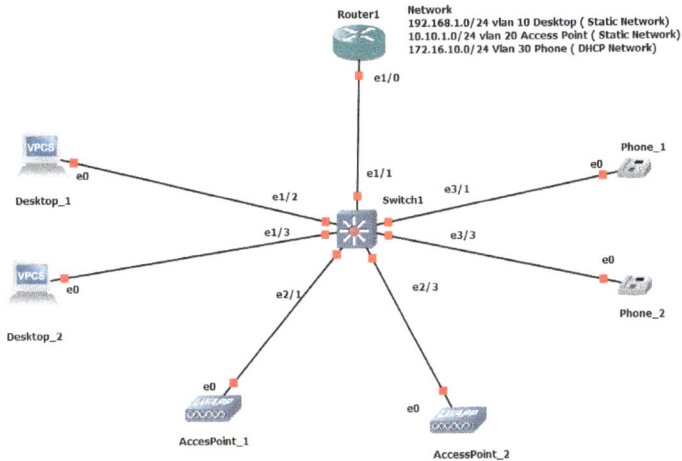

Global Configuration

1. Configure the hostname base on the Network Diagram.
2. Disable the DNS lookup feature.
3. Assign IKE as the secret password.
4. Direct the Cisco IOS to encrypt any passwords stored in clear text.

Console Port

5. Configure the console port on all devices to log input synchronously.
6. Set the password to NPTC.
7. Configure the idling timeout to 1 hour and 30 mins.

VTY Ports

8. Allow 5 concurrent sessions of remote access.
9. Configure the vty ports to log input synchronously.
10. Set password to V.
11. Configure idling timeout to 15 minutes and 10 seconds.
12. Save config.

Verify config

13. Assign an IP address to the router and describe the port and network.

Verify config

14. Configure the router to act as a DHCP Server and exclude 10 IP addresses from the Phone Scope.

Verify config

Show run | begin DHCP

Verify config

15. Configure VLAN on the switch and name it as stated on the topology.
16. Configure the switch virtual interface (SVI) using VLAN 10 on the switch.
17. Configure a Switch Default Gateway.

Verify config

18. Configure the Trunk Port to the port connected to the router and describe the port connections.

Verify config

19. Assign a VLAN to all connected devices base on the Network topology.

Verify config

20. Obtain the DHCP address from the connected DHCP Network and manually configure the static devices.

Lab Objective

Ensure communication among the entire device.

ROUTING

Routing is the process of sending packets from a host on one network to another host on a different remote network. This process is usually done by routers. Routers examine the destination IP address of a packet, determine the next-hop address, and forward the packet. Routers use routing tables to determine the next hop address to which the packet should be forwarded.

ROUTING PROTOCOLS

These are protocols that help Routing Protocols carry their information from one router to another example, **static routing** and **dynamic routing**, such as OSPF, EIGRP, RIP, and BGP, to figure out what paths traffic should take.

STATIC ROUTING

Static routing is a method of configuring routes in a network where network paths are manually defined by the network administrator. Unlike dynamic routing, static routes do not change automatically based on network conditions.

Advantages:

Static routes offer simplicity, lower resource usage, enhanced security, and predictable traffic paths in stable network environments.

Disadvantages:

Static routing can be cumbersome in larger, dynamic networks due to the manual configuration effort, and it lacks the automatic adaptation to network changes seen in dynamic routing.

Static Routing LAB TASK # 4

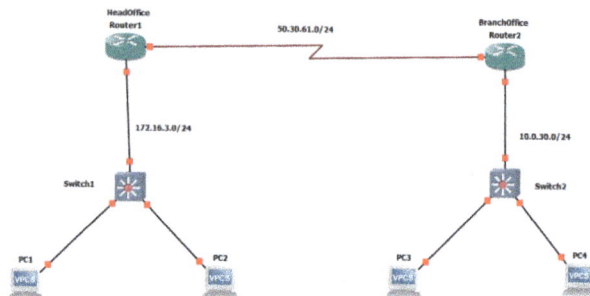

Global Configuration

1. Configure the hostname base on the Network Diagram.
2. Disable the DNS lookup feature.
3. Assign IKE as the Secret password.
4. Direct the Cisco IOS to encrypt any passwords stored in clear text.

Console Port

5. Configure the console port on all devices to log input synchronously.
6. Set the password to NPTC.
7. Configure the idling timeout to 1 hour and 30 mins.

VTY Ports

8. Allow 5 concurrent sessions of remote access.
9. Configure the vty ports to log input synchronously.
10. Set password to V.
11. Configure idling timeout to 15 minutes and 10 seconds.
12. Save config.
Verify the above steps using the proper Show command

13. Assigning IP addresses and port description
Verify the above steps using the proper Show command

- Show IP int br on the router

- Show run int (based on the topology)

14. Configure the Branch Office to act as a DHCP Server and exclude 10 IP addresses from the VLAN 20 Scope.

VLAN and Trunk

15. Configure VLAN 10 on Switch 1
16. Configure VLAN 20 on Switch 2
17. Configure the switch virtual interface (SVI) using the respective VLAN on the Switch.
18. Configure a Switch Default Gateway
19. Configure the Trunk Port base on the topology
20. Configure the Access port base on the topology
21. Disable all ports on the switches that are not connected

Verify the above steps using the proper Show command

- Show VLAN brief
- Show int trunk
- Show int status

Lab Objective

Ensure communication among all devices.

Static Routing

Configuration Example for Static Routes

10.0.3.0 = destination network

Configuration using next hope address

255.255.255.0 = subnet mask

50.30.61.2 = next-hop address

Headoffice (config)#IP route 10.0.30.0 255.255.255.0 50.30.61.2

To get to the destination network of 10.0.30.0, with a subnet mask of 255.255.255.0, send all packets to 50.30.61.2

10.0.30.0 = destination network

255.255.255.0 = subnet mask

S3/1 = exit interface

Configuration Using Exiting Interface

Read this to say: To get to the destination network of 10.0.30.0, with a subnet mask of 255.255.255.0, send all packets out interface Serial 3/1

Headoffice(config)#IP route 10.0.30.0 255.255.255.0 s3/1

Configuration using next hope address

To get to the destination network of 172.16.3.0, with a subnet mask of 255.255.255.0, send all packets to 50.30.61.1

Branchoffice(config)#IP route 172.16.3.0 255.255.255.0 50.30.61.1

Configuration Using Exiting Interface

Branchoffice(config)#IP route
172.16.3.0 255.255.255.0
s3/2

172.16.3.0 = destination network

255.255.255.0 = subnet mask

S3/2 = exit interface

Read this to say: To get to the destination network of 172.16.3.0, with a subnet mask of 255.255.255.0, send all packets out interface Serial 3/1

Router # show IP route.

When using the **Show IP route** command, you can identify where packets should be routed in two ways:

- The next-hop address
- The exit interface

Headoffice# show IP route.

Codes: C - connected, S - static, R - RIP, M - mobile, B - BGP

   D - EIGRP, EX - EIGRP external, O - OSPF, IA - OSPF inter area

   N1 - OSPF NSSA external type 1, N2 - OSPF NSSA external type 2

   E1 - OSPF external type 1, E2 - OSPF external type 2

i - IS-IS, su - IS-IS summary, L1 - IS-IS level-1, L2 - IS-IS level-2

   o - ODR, P - periodic downloaded static route

The Gateway of last resort is not set

   50.0.0.0/28 is subnetted, 1 subnet

C   50.30.60.48 is directly connected, Serial3/1

   10.0.0.0/24 is subnetted, 1 subnet

S   10.0.3.0 [1 /0] via 50.30.60.52

DEFAULT ROUTING

Configure Default Routing using project # 4

Remove the Static route and define a default route.

Head office (config) #no IP route 10.0.3.0 255.255.255.0 s3/1

Default Route

A default route is used by the router to forward traffic from unknown destinations to other routers.

Configuration using next hop address

Headoffice(config)#**IP route** 0.0.0.0 0.0.0.0 50.30.61.2

Send all packets destined for networks not in my routing table to **50.30.61.2**

Configuration Using Exiting Interface

Router(config)#**IP route** 0.0.0.0 0.0.0.0 s3/1

Send all packets destined for networks not in my routing table out to my Serial 3/1 interface.

Branchoffice(config)#**IP route** 0.0.0.0 0.0.0.0 50.30.61.1

Send all packets destined for networks not in my routing table to **50.30.61.1**

Router(config)#**IP route** 0.0.0.0 0.0.0.0 s3/2

Send all packets destined for networks not in my routing table out my Serial 3/1 interface.

Interview Questions for Practice

IQ: Define Static Routing.

IQ: What is Default Route?

IQ: What is Routing Protocol?

STATIC TASK #5

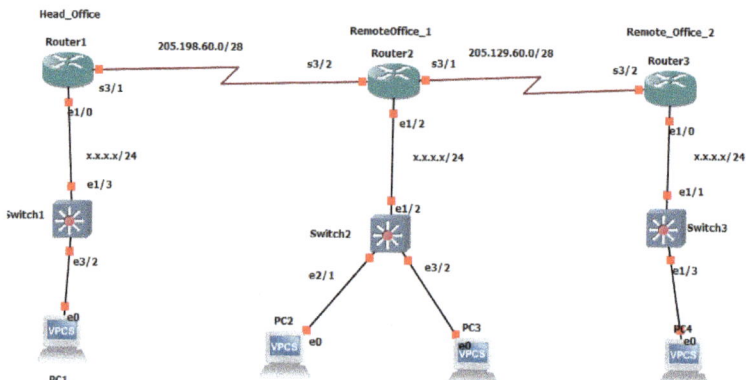

Global Configuration

1. Configure the hostname base on the Network Diagram.
2. Disable the DNS lookup feature.
3. Assign IKE as the Secret password.
4. Direct the Cisco IOS to encrypt any passwords stored in clear text.

Console Port

5. Configure the console port on all devices to log input synchronously.
6. Set the password to NPTC.
7. Configure the idling timeout to 1 hour and 30 minutes.

VTY Ports

8. Allow 5 concurrent sessions of remote access.
9. Configure the vty ports to log input synchronously.
10. Set password to V.
11. Configure idling timeout to 15 minutes and 10 seconds.
12. Save config.

Verify the above steps using the proper Show command.

Assigning IP Addresses and port description

- Choose your own local IP addresses for all the devices base on the topology.

Verify the above steps using the proper Show command.

- Configure the Remoteoffice_1 to act as a DHCP Server and exclude 10 IP addresses from the VLAN 200 Scope.

VLAN and Trunk

1. Configure VLAN 100 named Accounts on Switch1
2. Configure VLAN 200 Name as Stores on Switch 2
3. Configure VLAN 300 Name as Production on Switch 3
4. Configure the Trunk Port base on the topology
5. Configure the switch virtual interface (SVI) using the respective VLAN on the Switch.
6. Configure a Switch Default Gateway
7. Configure the Access port base on the topology
8. Disable all ports on the switches that are not connected.
9. Save Config

Verify the above steps using the proper Show command

- Configure the Static route Base on the topology

Verify the above steps using the proper Show command

Lab Objective

Ensure communication among all devices.

STATIC LAB ASSIGNMENT

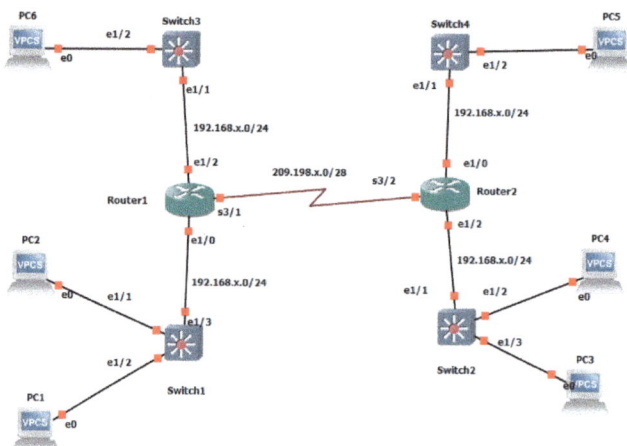

Global Configuration

1. Configure the hostname base on the Network Diagram.
2. Disable the DNS lookup feature.
3. Assign E as the Secret password.
4. Direct the Cisco IOS to encrypt any passwords stored in clear text.

Console Port

5. Configure the console port on all devices to log input synchronously.
6. Set password to NP.
7. Configure the idling timeout to 2 hours and 30 minutes.

VTY Ports

8. Allow 5 concurrent sessions of remote access.
9. Configure the vty ports to log input synchronously.
10. Set password to V.
11. Configure idling timeout to 15 minutes and 20 seconds.

Verify the above steps using the proper Show command.

- Assign IP addresses to all the devices base on the topology.

Verify the above steps using the proper Show command

- Configure the Site_2 router to act as a DHCP Server and exclude 10 IP addresses from the VLAN 104 Scope

VLAN and Trunk

1. Configure VLAN 101 Name as Accounts on Switch1
2. Configure VLAN 102 Name as Directors on Switch 2
3. Configure VLAN 103 on switch 3
4. Configure VLAN 104 on switch 4
5. Configure the Trunk Port base on the topology
6. Configure the Access port base on the topology
7. Disable all ports on the switches that are not connected.
8. Save Config

Verify the above steps using the proper Show command

- Configure the Static route Base on the topology

ENHANCED INTERIOR GATEWAY ROUTING PROTOCOL (EIGRP)

Enhanced Interior Gateway Routing Protocol (EIGRP) is an advanced distance-vector routing protocol that is used on a computer network for automating routing decisions and configuration. The protocol was designed by Cisco Systems as a proprietary protocol, available only on Cisco routers.

It is a Cisco proprietary protocol, so all routers in a network that is running EIGRP must be Cisco routers.

EIGPR uses the concept of autonomous systems. An autonomous system is a set of EIGRP-enabled routers that should become EIGRP neighbors. Each router inside an autonomous system must have the same autonomous system number configured; otherwise, routers will not become neighbors.

EIGRP Neighbors

EIGRP must establish neighbor relationships with other EIGRP neighboring routers before exchanging routing information. To establish neighbor relationships, routers send hello packets every couple of seconds. Hello packets are sent to the multicast address of 224.0.0.10.

NOTE

On LAN interfaces, hellos are sent every 5 seconds. On WAN interfaces every 60 seconds.

Routers send hello packets every couple of seconds to ensure that the neighbor relationship is still active. By default, a router considers the neighbor to be down after a hold-down timer has expired. The hold-down timer is, by default, three times the hello interval. On the LAN network, the hold-down timer is 15 seconds.

SHOW COMMAND (EIGRP)

- **Show run | begin router** – shows the real configuration of the eigrp
- **Show IP route** – display summary information about all routes for the specified protocol.
- **Show IP eigrp neighbor**- The neighbor table keeps a record of the IP addresses of routers that have a direct physical connection with this router.

EIGRP LAB # 6

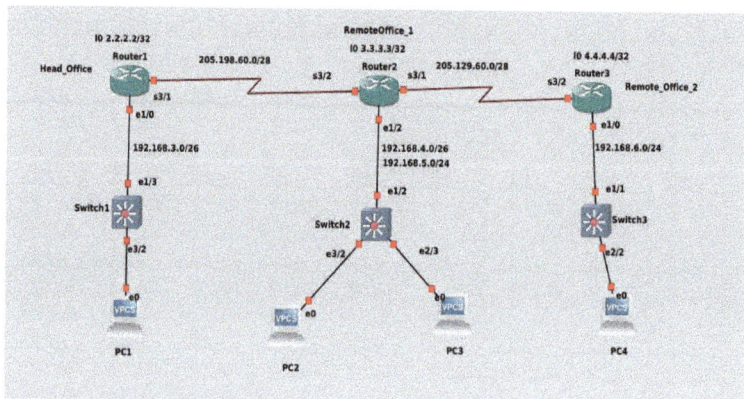

Global Configuration

1. Configure the hostname as follows.

R1-HeadOffice
R2-RemoteOffice_1
R3-RemoteOffice_2

2. Disable the DNS lookup feature.
3. Assign RING as the Secret password.
4. Direct the Cisco IOS to encrypt any passwords stored in clear text.

Console Port

5. Configure the console port on all devices to log input synchronously.
6. Set password to PTC.
7. Configure the idling timeout to 40 minutes and 30 seconds.

VTY Ports

8. Allow 5 concurrent sessions of remote access.
9. Configure the vty ports to log input synchronously.
10. Set the password to CR.
11. Configure idling timeout to 60 mins and 60 secs.
12. Save config.

- Assign the IP address and port description based on the topology and verify the interface.

Verify if the IP interface is up and can ping each other.

- Configure the RemoteOffice_1 to act as DHCP Server and exclude 10 IP addresses from the VLAN 200 Scope.
- Configure the VLAN below and assign it to the respective PCs.

Switch1 - VLAN 100
Switch2 - VLAN 200 and 300
Switch3 - VLAN 400

- Create the loopback interface on all the routers.

LOOPBACK INTERFACE/ADDRESSES

A loopback interface is a **logical**, **virtual** interface in a Cisco Router. A loopback interface is not a physical interface like a Fast Ethernet interface or a Gigabit Ethernet interface.

The loopback interface is used to identify the device. While any interface address can be used to determine if the device is online, the loopback address is the preferred method. Whereas interfaces might be removed or addresses changed based on network topology changes, the loopback address never changes.

When you ping an individual interface address, the results do not always indicate the health of the device.

Loopback Configuration Guide

WorcesterRouter **# conf t**

WorcesterRouter **(config)# int l0**

WorcesterRouter **(config)# IP add** 2.2.2.2 255.255.255.255

NatickRouter **# conf t**

NatickRouter **(config)# int l0**

NatickRouter **(config)# IP add** 3.3.3.3 255.255.255.255

BostonRouter**# conf t**

BostonRouter**(config)# int l0**

BostonRouter(config)# IP add 4.4.4.4 255.255.255.255

- Configure all the routers with the EIGRP using (autonomous system) AS 100

Verify your config with the following show command

1. Verify EIGRP neighbors

Verify EIGRP learned routes and connectivity

EIGRP Configuration Guide

WorcesterRouter# configure terminal
WorcesterRouter(config)# router eigrp 100
WorcesterRouter(config-router)# network 2.2.2.2 0.0.0.0
WorcesterRouter(config-router)# network 192.168.3.0 0.0.0.63
WorcesterRouter(config-router)# network 205.198.60.0 0.0.0.15
WorcesterRouter(config-router)# no auto-summary
WorcesterRouter(config-router)# exit

NatickRouter# configure terminal.
NatickRouter(config)# router eigrp 100
NatickRouter(config-router)# network 3.3.3.3 0.0.0.0
NatickRouter(config-router)# network 192.168.4.0 0.0.0.63
NatickRouter(config-router)# network 192.168.5.0 0.0.0.63
NatickRouter(config-router)# network 205.200.60.0 0.0.0.15
NatickRouter(config-router)# network 205.198.60.0 0.0.0.15
NatickRouter(config-router)# no auto-summary
NatickRouter(config-router)# exit

BostonRouter# configure terminal
Boston(config)# router eigrp 100
BostonRouter(config-router)# network 4.4.4.4 0.0.0.0
BostonRouter(config-router)# network 192.168.6.0 0.0.0.63
BostonRouter(config-router)# network 205.200.60.0 0.0.0.15
BostonRouter(config-router)# no auto-summary
BostonRouter(config-router)# exit

Verify your config with the following show command

- Show IP route – display summary information about all routes for the specified protocol.
- Show IP eigrp neighbor- The neighbor table keeps a record of the IP addresses of routers that have a direct physical connection with this router.

EIGRP automatic & manual summarization

Route summarization is a method of representing multiple networks with a single summary address. It is often used in large networks with many subnets because it reduces the number of routes that a router must maintain and minimizes the traffic used for routing updates. Two methods for summarizing routes exist: automatic summarization and manual summarization.

EIGRP AUTOMATIC SUMMARIZATION

By default, EIGRP has the auto-summary feature enabled. Because of this, routes are summarized to classful addresses at network boundaries in the routing updates.

The manual summarization in EIGRP is configured on a per-interface basis. The syntax of the command is:

(config-if)IP summary-address eigrp ASN SUMMARY_ADDRESS SUBNET_MASK

So, if we want to summarize the route on Router 1, the configuration should be done on Router 2, with the interface going to Router 1.

NatickRouter# configure terminal

#Int s3/2

#IP summary-address eigrp 100   192.168.0.0 255.255.0.0

Interview Questions

IQ: Why is no auto-summary command used in EIGRP?

IQ: How do we configure EIGRP?

IQ: Give some commands to troubleshoot EIGRP.

IQ: What is AD for EIGRP?

EIGRP ASSIGNMENT

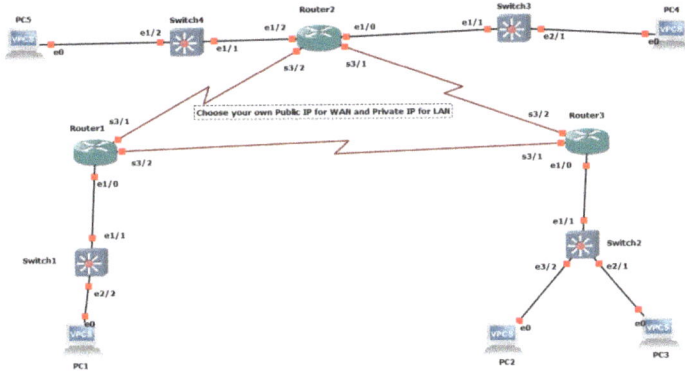

Global Configuration

1. Configure the hostname base as follows.

R1 - Router_1
R2-Router_2
R3-Router_3

2. Disable the DNS lookup feature.
3. Assign RING as the Secret password.
4. Direct the Cisco IOS to encrypt any passwords stored in clear-text

Console Port

5. Configure the console port on all devices to log input synchronously
6. Set password to TC
7. Configure the idling timeout to 20 minutes and 20 seconds

VTY Ports

8. Allow 5 concurrent sessions of remote access
9. Configure the vty ports to log input synchronously
10. Set password to CR
11. Save config

- Assign IP address and port description based on the topology and use your own public IP addresses on WAN.

Verify if the IP interfaces are up and can ping each other.

- Configure all the routers with the EIGRP using autonomous system (AS) 400

Verify your config with the following show command

Verify EIGRP neighbors

Verify EIGRP topology

Verify EIGRP learned routes and connectivity

Lab Objective

Ensure communication among all devices.

OPEN SHORTEST PATH FIRST (OSPF)

Open Shortest Path First (OSPF) is a routing protocol for Internet Protocol (IP) networks. It uses a link-state routing (LSR) algorithm and falls into the group of interior gateway protocols (IGPs) operating within a single autonomous system (AS). It is defined as OSPF Version 2 for IPv4. The updates for IPv6 are specified as OSPF Version 3.

OSPF is an open standard industry protocol, which can also be used with non-Cisco devices like Juniper.

Routers running OSPF have to establish neighbor relationships before exchanging routes. Because OSPF is a link-state routing protocol, neighbors don't exchange routing tables. Instead, they exchange information about network topology.

By default, OSPF sends hello packets every 10 seconds on an Ethernet network (Hello interval). A dead timer is four times the value of the hello interval, so if a router on an Ethernet network doesn't receive at least one Hello packet from an OSPF neighbor for 40 seconds, the router declares that neighbor to be down.

OSPF areas

OSPF uses the concept of areas. An area is a logical grouping of contiguous networks and routers. All routers in the same area have the same topology table, but they don't know about routers in the other areas. The main benefits of creating areas are that the size of the topology and the routing table on a router is reduced, less time is required to run the SFP algorithm, and routing updates are also reduced.

Each area in the OSPF network has to connect to the backbone area (area 0). All routers inside an area must have the same area ID to become OSPF neighbors. A router that has interfaces in more than one area (area 0 and area 1, for example) is called an **Area Border Router (ABR)**. A router that connects an OSPF network to other routing domains (EIGRP network, for example) is called an **Autonomous System Border Router (ASBR)**.

NOTE

In OSPF, manual route summarization is possible only on ABRs and ASBRs.

What is the difference between EIGRP and OSPF?

The following table lists the differences between OSPF and EIGRP:

Protocol	EIGRP	OSPF
Type of Routing	Advanced distance vector protocol of bandwidth and delay	Link state
Metric	Com	cost
Manual Summarization	On all routers	Only on ABRs and ASBDRs
Load Balancing	Equal and unequal cost load balancing	Equal cost load balancing
Administrative Distance	90	110
Cisco Propriety	Yes	No
Multcast Address	224.0.0.10	224.0,0,5, 224.0.6

OSPF LAB #7

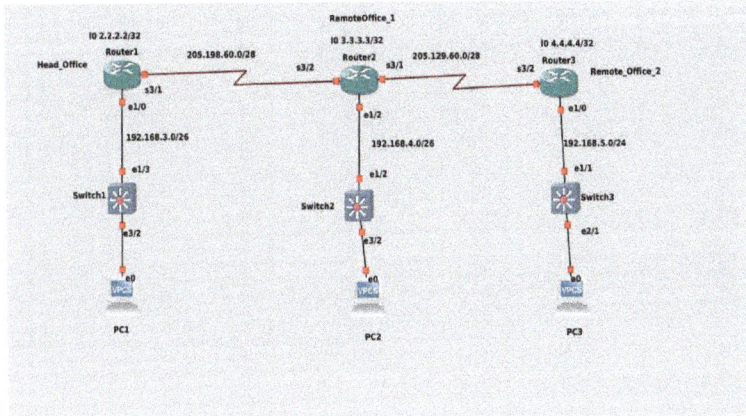

Global Configuration

1. Configure the hostname as follows

R1 - HeadOffice
R2-Remote_Office_1
R3-Remote_Office_2

2. Disable the DNS lookup feature.
3. Assign RING as the Secret password.
4. Direct the Cisco IOS to encrypt any passwords stored in clear text.

Console Port

5. Configure the console port on all devices to log input synchronously.
6. Set password to PTC.
7. Configure the idling timeout to 40 minutes and 30 seconds.

VTY Ports

8. Allow 5 concurrent sessions of remote access.
9. Configure the vty ports to log input synchronously.
10. Set password to CR.
11. Configure idling timeout to 60 minutes and 60 seconds.
12. Save config.

Assigning IP Addresses

- Assign an IP address to describe the port base on the topology and verify the interface.

Verify if the IP interfaces are up and can ping each other.

- Configure all the routers with the OSPF using AS 10 and Area 100.

Configuration Guide

Router_R1(config)#router OSPF 10

Network 2.2.2.2 0.0.0.0 area 100
Network 192.168.3.0 0.0.0.63 area 100
Network 205.198.60.0 0.0.0.15 area 100

Router_R2 (config)#router OSPF 10

Network 3.3.3.3 0.0.0.0 area 100
Network 192.168.4.0 0.0.0.63 area 100
Network 205.198.60.0 0.0.0.15 area 100
#Network 205.200.60.0 0.0.0.15 area 100

Router_R3(config)#**router OSPF** 10

Network 4.4.4.4 0.0.0.0 area 100
Network 192.168.5.0 0.0.0.63 area 100
Network 205.200.60.0 0.0.0.15 area 100

Verify your config with the following show command

Show run | sec OSPF

Show IP OSPF neighbors

Interview Questions

QI: What is the OSPF routing protocol?

QI: Mention some characteristics of OSPF.

QI: What is the benefit of dividing the entire network into areas?

QI: What is the Backbone Area?

Q1: Explain ABR.

OSPF ASSIGNMENT

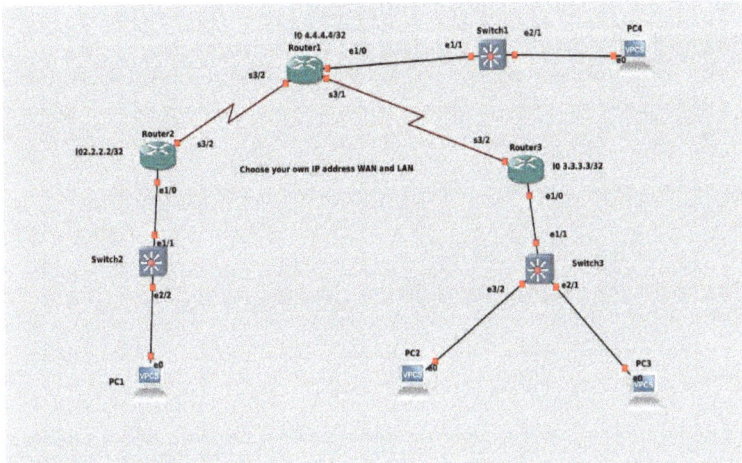

Global Configuration

1. Configure the hostname base on the Network Diagram.
2. Disable the DNS lookup feature.
3. Assign IKE as the Secret password.
4. Direct the Cisco IOS to encrypt any passwords stored in clear text.

Console Port

5. Configure the console port on all devices to log input synchronously.
6. Set password to N.
7. Configure the idling timeout to 1 hour and 30 mins.

VTY Ports

8. Allow 5 concurrent sessions of remote access
9. Configure the vty ports to log input synchronously
10. Set password to R
11. Configure idling timeout to 40 mins and 10 secs
12. Save config

Verify the above steps using the proper Show command

VLAN and Trunk

13. Configure VLAN 10 Name as head office on Switch1

14. Configure VLAN 20 Name as Stores on Switch 2
15. Configure VLAN 30 Name as Accounts on Switch 3
16. Configure the Trunk Port base on the topology
17. Configure the Access port base on the topology
18. Disable all ports on the switches that are not connected.
19. Save Config

Verify the above steps using the proper Show command

Assigning IP Addresses

• Assign IP addresses to all the devices base on the topology.

Verify the above steps using the proper Show command

• Configure all the routers with OSPF using AS 100 and Area 50

Verify the above steps using the proper Show command

Lab Objective

Ensure communication among all the devices.

OSPF with Multi-Area

You can have multiple areas to contain your routing updates within your area; thereby, the OSPF database would be smaller, resulting in faster convergence. If there is a link instability in your area, that will not disturb other areas if you have multiple areas.

Summarization is also a very big benefit of this structure, and everyone should consider making their networks contiguous.

LAB TASK 8

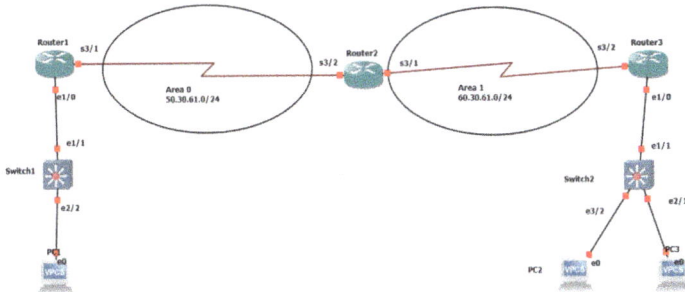

Global Configuration

1. Configure the hostname as follows
   R1- Russia_Router
   R2-China_Router
   R3-UK_Router
   EWS1- Russia_Switch
   ESW2- UK_Switch

2. Disable the DNS lookup feature.
3. Assign Pa$$ as the Secret password.
4. Direct the Cisco IOS to encrypt any passwords stored in cleartext.

Console Port

5. Configure the console port on all devices to log input synchronously
6. Set password to w0rd
7. Configure the idling timeout to 1 hour and 30 mins

VTY Ports

8. Allow 5 concurrent sessions of remote access
9. Configure the VTY ports to log input synchronously
10. Set password to 100k
11. Configure idling timeout to 15 minutes and 10 seconds
12. Save config

Verify the above steps using the proper Show command

VLAN and Trunk

1. Configure VLAN 450 on Russia_Switch and name it as Data
2. Configure VLANs 20 and 10 on UK_switch and name them as Data and Voice, respectively
3. Configure the Trunk Port base on the topology
4. Configure the Access port base on the topology by using VLAN 10 for port 2 and VLAN 20 for port 1
5. Disable all ports on the switches that are not connected.

Verify the above steps using the proper Show command

Assigning IP Addresses

- Assign IP addresses to all the devices and describe the port base on the topology.

Verify the above steps using the proper Show command

- Show IP int br on the Router
- Show IP on the PC

DHCP Server

- Configure the Russia routers as a DHCP server using the respective network.

Verify by obtaining the DHCP IP address on all the PCs

OSPF Network

- Configure OSPF on the entire router using AS 20

Verify the above steps using the proper Show command

Configure the route on the border router using the respective area

Configuration Guide for Multi-Area System

China_Router (Config) # router OSPF 20

    # Network 50.30.61.0 0.0.0.255 area 0

    # Network 60.30.61.0 0.0.0.255 area 1

OSPF summarization

Route summarization helps reduce OSPF traffic and route computation. OSPF, unlike EIGRP, doesn't support automatic summarization. Also, unlike EIGRP, where you can summarize routes on every router in an EIGRP network, OSPF can summarize routes only on ABRs and ASBRs.

The following command is used for OSPF summarization:

(config-router) area AREA_ID range IP_ADDRESS MASK

So, if we want to summarize the route on Router 1, the configuration should be done on Router 2

China_Router (Config) # router OSPF 20

    # area 1 range 172.16.0.0 255.255.0.0

REDISTRIBUTION OF PROTOCOLS

Route redistribution is when you take a **route** from one **routing** protocol and distribute it into another protocol. By default, routers only advertise and share **routes** with other routers running the same protocol.

Small companies mostly run one routing protocol like OSPF, EIGRP, or static as the company gets bigger and buys more than one company that runs different protocols. Then, you will need to redistribute your route.

Redistribution Configuration for different EIGRP AS Numbers

Router eigrp 100

Redistribute eigrp 200

Router eigrp 200

redistributeeigrp100

Redistribution Configuration for different OSPF AS Number

Router OSPF 1

Redistribute OSPF 2 subnet

Router OSPF 2

Redistribute OSPF 1 subnet

Redistribution Configuration with mixed OSPF & EIGRP Environment

Router OSPF 1

Redistribute eigrp 500 subnets

Router eigrp 500

Redistribute OSPF 1 metric 5000 10 255 255 65535

Redistribution configuration with default route and EIGRP

IP route 0.0.0.0 0.0.0.0 s3/1

router eigrp 1

redistribute static

Redistribution configuration with default route and OSPF

IP route 0.0.0.0 0.0.0.0 s3/1

router OSPF 1

default-information originate

REDISTRIBUTION PROJECT

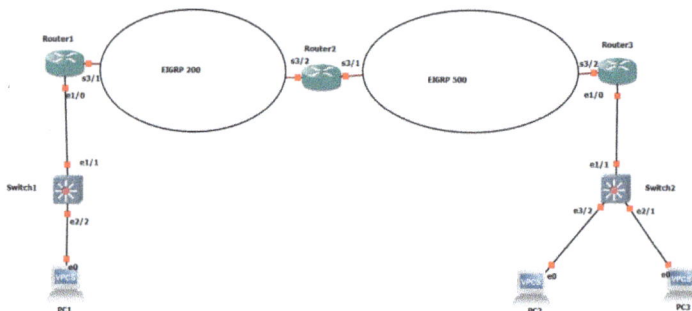

Global Configuration

1. Configure the hostname as follows
   R1 - Singapore_Router
   R2-Germany_Router
   R3-Worcester_Router
   EWS1 - Singapore_Switch
   ESW2- Worcester_Switch

2. Disable the DNS lookup feature.
3. Assign Pa$$w0rd as the Secret password.
4. Direct the Cisco IOS to encrypt any passwords stored in clear text.

Console Port

5. Configure the console port on all devices to log input synchronously
6. Set password to W0rd
7. Configure the idling timeout to 1 hour and 30 minutes

VTP Ports

8. Allow 5 concurrent sessions of remote access
9. Configure the VTY ports to log input synchronously
10. Set the password to Vod
11. Configure idling timeout to 15 minutes and 10 seconds
12. Save config

Verify the above steps using the proper Show command

VLAN and Trunk

13.Configure VLAN 10 on Worcester_Switch and name it Data

14.Configure VLAN 20 on Singapore_switch and name it Data

15.Configure the Trunk Port base on the topology

16.Configure the Access port base on the topology

17.Disable all ports on the switches that are not connected.

Verify the above steps using the proper Show command

Assigning IP Addresses

- Assign your own IP addresses to create a network for all the devices and describe the port base on the topology.

Verify the above steps using the proper Show command

- Show IP int br on the Router
- Show IP on the PC

DHCP Server

- Configure both routers as DHCP servers using their respective Network and reserved 10 IPs

Verify by obtaining the DHCP IP address on all the PCs

- Configure EIGRP on both sides and redistribute the different AS numbers base on the topology

Verify the above steps using the proper Show command

BORDER GATEWAY PROTOCOL (BGP)

BGP stands for Border Gateway Protocol, and it is the main dynamic routing protocol used on the Internet. BGP is for large networks and is normally used for connecting different ISPs.

The Border Gateway Protocol makes routing decisions based on paths, network policies, or rule sets configured by a network administrator and is involved in making core routing decisions.

When BGP runs between two peers in the same autonomous system (AS), it is referred to as *Internal BGP* (iBGP or Interior Border Gateway Protocol). When it runs between different autonomous systems, it is called *External BGP* (eBGP or Exterior Border Gateway Protocol). Routers on the boundary of one AS exchanging information with another AS are called *border* or *edge routers* or simply eBGP *peers* and are typically connected directly.

BGP LAB #10

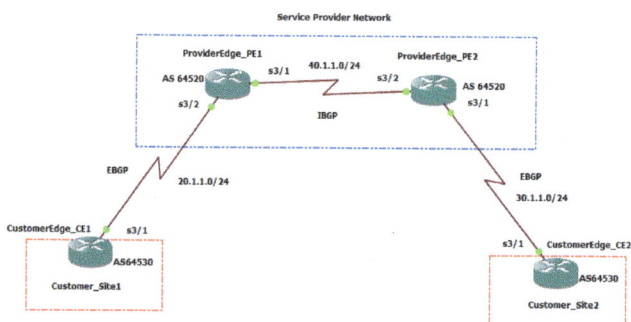

Customer Edge (CE) router sits at the edge of a customer site and is typically owned by the customer.

Provider Edge (PE) router sits at the edge of the provider's network, connecting one or several CE routers.

Global Configuration

1. Configure the hostname
2. Disable the DNS lookup feature.
3. Assign Pa$$w0rd as the Secret password.
4. Direct the Cisco IOS to encrypt any passwords stored in clear text.

Console Port

5. Configure the console port on all devices to log input synchronously
6. Set password to Pass
7. Configure the idling timeout to 1 hour and 0 minutes

VTP Ports

8. Allow 5 concurrent sessions of remote access
9. Configure the VTY ports to log input synchronously
10. Set password to Pass
11. Configure idling timeout to 20 minutes and 10 seconds
12. Save config

Verify the above steps using the proper Show command.

- Assign an IP address to describe the port base on the topology and verify the interface.

Verify if the IP interfaces are up and can ping each other

Configuration Guide for BGP

PE1 Router

ProviderEdge_PE1(config)# **router bgp** 64520
ProviderEdge_PE1(config-router)#**neighbor** 40.1.1.2 **remote-as** 64520
ProviderEdge_PE1(config-router)#**neighbor** 20.1.1.2 **remote-as** 64530

PE2 Router

ProviderEdge_PE2(config)# **router bgp** 64520
ProviderEdge_PE2(config-router)#**neighbor** 40.1.1.1 **remote-as** 64520
ProviderEdge_PE2(config-router)#**neighbor** 30.1.1.1 **remote-as** 64530

CE1 Router

CustomerEdge_CE1(config)# **router bgp** 64530
CustomerEdge_CE1(config-router)#**neighbor** 20.1.1.1 **remote-as** 64520

CE2 Router

CustomerEdge_CE2(config-if)# router bgp 64530
CustomerEdge_CE2(config-router)#neighbor 30.1.1.2 **remote-as** 64520

Show command for BGP

- Show run | sec bgp
- show IP bgp
- show IP bgp summary
- show IP bgp neighbors

ProviderEdge_PE1#show IP bgp summary.

BGP router identifier 40.1.1.1, local AS number 64520

The BGP table version is 1, and the main routing table version is 1

Neighbor	20.1.1.2	40.1.1.2
V	4	4
AS	64530	64520
MsgRcvd	23	16
MsgSent	23	17

TblVer	1	1
InQ	0	0
OutQ	0	0
Up/Down	00:17:54	00:12:05
State/PfxRcd	0	0

Route Source	Administrative Distance Values
Connected interface	0
Static route	1
Enhanced Interior Gateway Routing Protocol (EIGRP) summary route	5
External Border Gateway Protocol (eBGP)	20
EIGRP	90
IGRP	100
OSPF	110
Intermediate System-to-Intermediate System (IS-IS)	115
Routing Information Protocol (RIP)	120
Internal BGP(iBGP)	200

REMOTE OFFICE SETUP WITH MULTILAYER SWITCH (LAYER3 SWITCH)

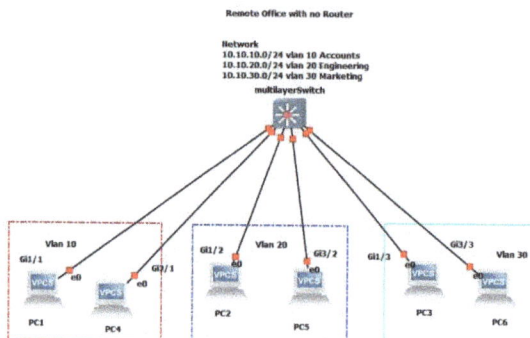

Global Configuration

1. Configure the hostname base on the topology
2. Disable the DNS lookup feature.
3. Assign Cisco as the Secret password.

Console Port

4. Configure the console port on all devices to log input synchronously
5. Set password to NPTC
6. Configure the idling timeout to 10 minutes and 20 minutes

VTY Ports

7. Allow 5 concurrent sessions of remote access
8. Configure the VTY ports to log input synchronously
9. Set password to Cisco
10. Configure idling timeout to 10 minutes and 60 seconds

VLAN Configuration

11. Configure VLAN 10, 20, and 30 and name them as Accounts, Engineering and Marketing VLAN, respectively

Trunk Configuration

12. Configure the trunk port base on the topology

Switch Virtual Interface (SVI)

A **Switched Virtual Interface** (SVI) represents a logical Layer 3 **interface** on a **switch**. VLANs divide broadcast domains in a LAN environment. Whenever hosts in one VLAN need to communicate with hosts in another VLAN, the traffic must be routed between them. This is known as inter-VLAN routing.

SVIs are generally configured for a VLAN for the following reasons:

- Allow traffic to be routed between VLANs by providing a default gateway for the VLAN.
- Provide Layer 3 IP connectivity to the switch.
- Support bridging configurations and routing protocol.

An SVI can also be known as a Routed VLAN Interface (RVI) by some vendors.

SVI Configuration

13. Configure all the switch virtual interface (SVI) to create your network

Switch (config)# **interface VLAN 10**
  # des Accounts
  # IP add 10.10.10.1 255.255.255.0
  # no shut

IP Addresses

14. Assign IP addresses to your PC based on the topology.

CORPORATE NETWORK INFRASTRUCTURE DESIGN

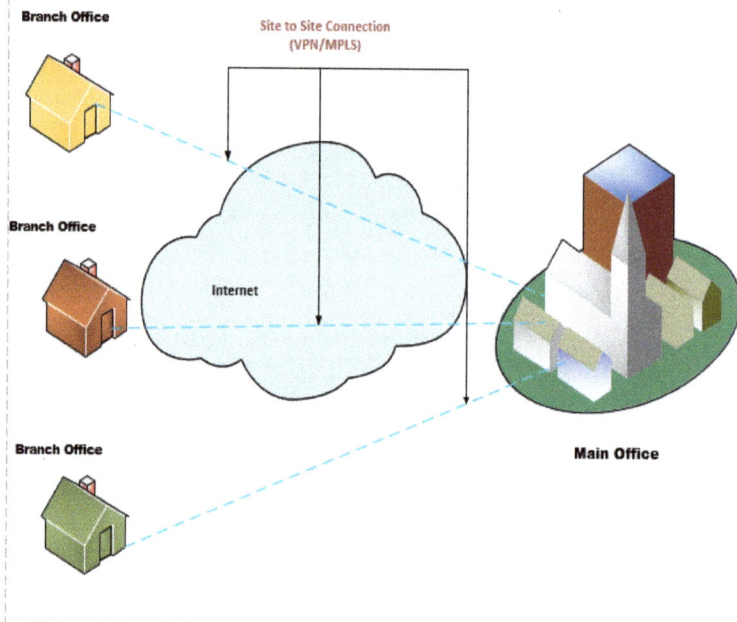

WIDE AREA NETWORK (WAN) TECHNOLOGY

Though WANs cover a wide area, connections can be either wired or wireless. Wired WANs usually consist of broadband internet services, cable modems, and multiprotocol label switching (MPLS), which is a form of data-forwarding technology used to control traffic flow and speed up the connection. While wireless WANs normally include 4G/5G and Long-Term Evolution (LTE) networks.

1. In an enterprise, a WAN is created to connect branch offices with one another or to connect remote employees working at home with the company's main office.
2. A bank, including its branch offices and ATM machines, is another example of an organization using a WAN. The branches may be in multiple U.S. states or even global locations, but they are all linked through various secure connections. Both bank employees and customers are users.
3. It can be said that the internet is the world's largest WAN because it's the largest and most diverse form of a computer network in the world.

Examples of Equipment use by ISPs for WAN Technology

ISP Modems technology- Cable modem, broadband modem, frame relay modem, DSL modem, T-1 modem, ATM modem (Mostly for VPN connections)

ISP Circuit technology – ELAN Circuit, MPLS Circuit (use as a dedicated line)

Controllers- SD-WAN (Software Defined Wide Area Network)

FRAME RELAY

A frame-relay is a wide area network technology (WAN) that provides packet-switching data communication capabilities that can be used across the interfaces between user devices and network equipment.

Devices

In order for a frame relay WAN to transmit data, data terminal equipment (DTE) and data circuit-terminating equipment (DCE) are required. DTEs are typically located on the customer's premises and can encompass terminals, routers, and bridges. DCEs are managed by the carriers and provide switching and associated services.

Point-to-Point Protocol

The Point to Point is used to establish a direct connection between two network devices. PPP is the most widely used WAN connection today because of its advanced features. Frame Relay utilizes a private virtual circuit (PVC) called a Data Link Connection Identifier (DLCI) to create paths.

Most ISPs use it in order to provide their customers access to the internet through dial-up connections, broadband connections, and DSL.

FRAME-RELAY(POINT-TO-POINT)

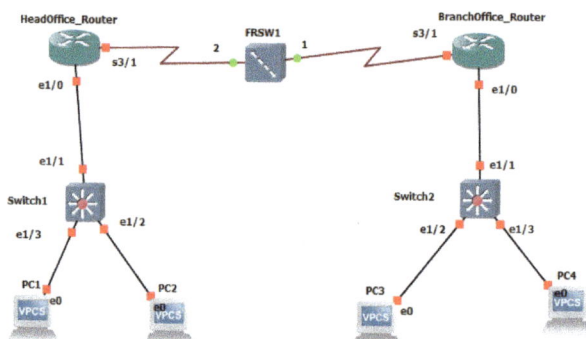

FRAME RELAY CONFIGURATION GUIDE

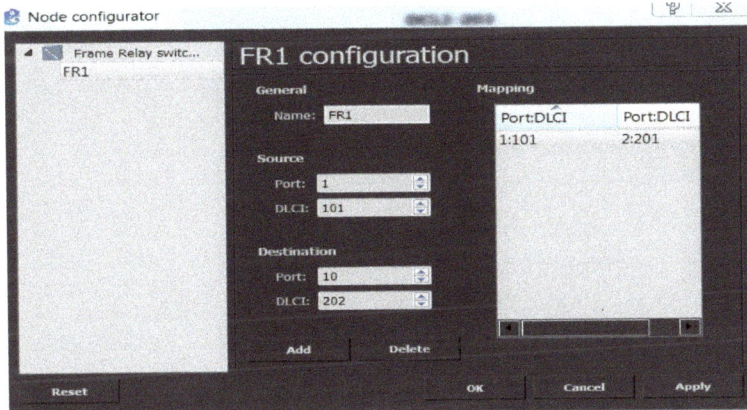

Global Configuration

1. Configure the hostname base on the topology
2. Disable the DNS lookup feature.
3. Assign Ring as the Secret password.

Console Port

4. Configure the console port on all devices to log input synchronously
5. Set password to NPTC
6. Configure the idling timeout to 10 minutes and 40 minutes

VTY Ports

7. Allow 16 concurrent sessions of remote access
8. Configure the VTY ports to log input synchronously
9. Set the password to CW2
10. Configure idling timeout to 20 minutes and 60 seconds
11. Save config

VLAN Configuration

12. Configure VLANs for the head office and branch office, respectively, and name them as Data on the switch base on the topology.
13. Assign access port and trunk port where necessary based on the Topology.

Network

14. Create a network for each of the offices base on the topology.
15. Assign static IP addresses for the PCs base on their respective network.
16. Configure frame encapsulation on a serial interface.

R1(config)#**int s3/1**
R1(config-if)#**no shut**
R1(config-if)#**encapsulation frame-relay**

R2(config)#**int s3/1**
R2(config-if)#**no shut**
R2(config-if)#**encapsulation frame-relay**

17. Configure Point-to-Point Protocol encapsulation and assign IP addresses using the DLCI on the topology.

R1(config)#**int s3/1.1 point-to-point**
R1(config-subif)#**IP address 20.20.1.1 255.255.255.0**
R1(config-subif)#**IP OSPF network point-to-point** (**Bring this only when you are using OSPF**)
R1(config-subif)#**frame-relay interface-dlci 201**

R2(config)#int s3/1.1 point-to-point
R2(config-subif)#IP address 20.20.1.2 255.255.255.0
R2(config-subif)#IP OSPF network point-to-point (Bring this only when you are using OSPF)
R2(config-subif)#frame-relay interface-dlci 101

Network Routing

18. Use the OSPF routing protocol to route your network from one destination to another.

Note: Remember, when configuring the frame-relay interface, make sure your destination DLCI is your local DLCI and not the remote one!

Verify Connectivity.

Test Verification Result

Ensure that all PCs can ping each other

FRAME-RELAY(POINT-TO-MULTIPOINT) PROJECT

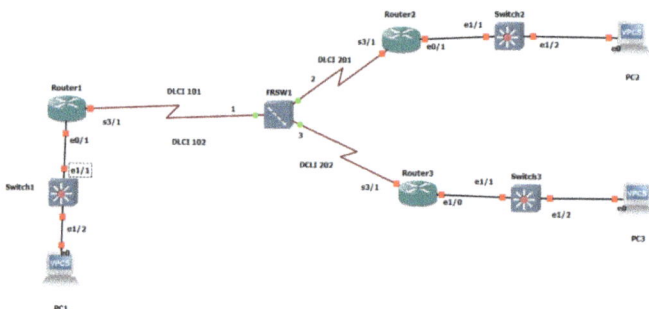

FRAME RELAY CONFIGURATION GUIDE

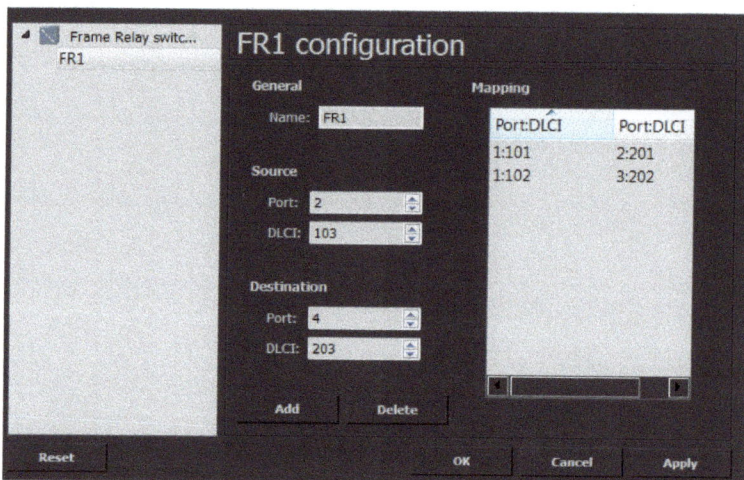

Global Configuration

1. Configure the hostname base on the topology.
2. Disable the DNS lookup feature.
3. Assign R"ng as the Secret password.

Console Port

4. Configure the console port on all devices to log input synchronously.
5. Set password to KU%%
6. Configure the idling timeout to 10 minutes and 40 minutes.

VTY Ports

7. Allow 16 concurrent sessions of remote access.
8. Configure the VTY ports to log input synchronously.
9. Set the password to C@2
10. Configure idling timeout to 40 minutes and 60 seconds.
11. Save config.
12. Configure frame encapsulation on a serial interface.
13. Configure Point to Multipoint Protocol encapsulation and assign IP addresses using the DLCI on the topology.

R1(config)#**int s3/1**
R1(config-if)#**no shut**
R1(config-if)#**encapsulation frame-relay**
R1(config)#**int s3/1.1 multiPoint**
R1(config-subif)#**IP address 20.20.1.1 255.255.255.0**
R1(config-subif)#**frame-relay map IP 20.20.1.2 101 broadcast**
R1(config-subif)#**frame-relay map IP 20.20.1.3 102 broadcast**

R2(config)#**int s3/1**
R2(config-if)#**no shut**
R2(config-if)#**encapsulation frame-relay**
R2(config)#**int s3/1.1 multiPoint**
R2(config-subif)#**IP address 20.20.1.2 255.255.255.0**
R2(config-subif)#**frame-relay map IP 20.20.1.1 201 broadcast**

R3(config)#**int s3/1**
R3(config-if)#**no shut**
R3(config-if)#**encapsulation frame-relay**
R3(config)#**int s3/1.1 multiPoint**
R3 (config-subif)#**IP address 20.20.1.3 255.255.255.0**
R3 (config-subif)#**frame-relay map IP 20.20.1.1 202 broadcast**

Note: Remember, when configuring maps, make sure your destination DLCI is your local DLCI and not the remote one!

Ping your neighbors to verify connectivity.

Network Routing

1. Use EIGRP to route your network from one destination to another.

Check for connectivity

FRAME-RELAY(MULTIPOINT) PROJECT TASK 7

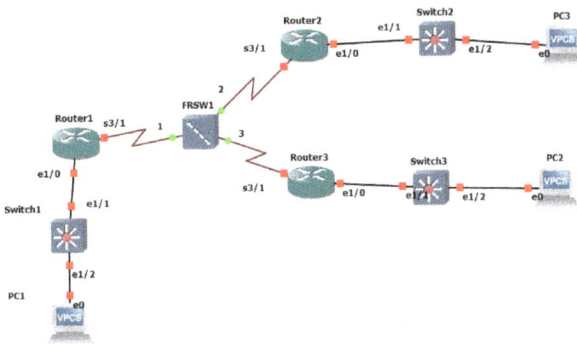

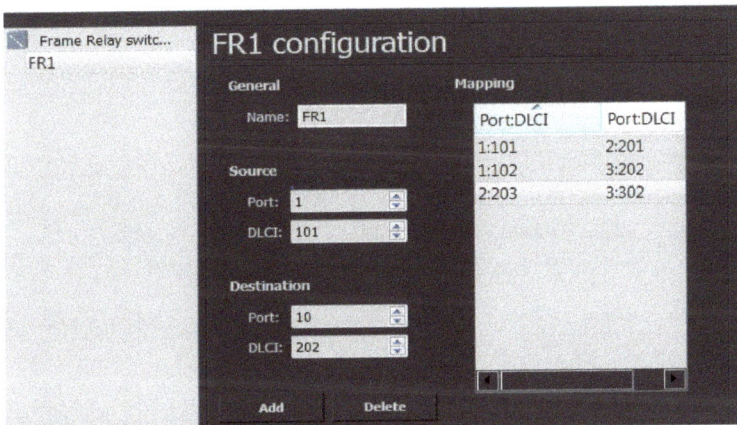

FR1 configuration

General		Mapping	
Name: FR1		Port:DLCI	Port:DLCI
		1:101	2:201
Source		1:102	3:202
Port: 1		2:203	3:302
DLCI: 101			
Destination			
Port: 10			
DLCI: 202			
Add	Delete		

Global Configuration

1. Configure a hostname for all the devices.
2. Disable the DNS lookup feature.
3. Assign R#ng as the Secret password.

Console Port

4. Configure the console port on all devices to log input synchronously.
5. Set the password to N@TC
6. Configure the idling timeout to 10 minutes and 40 minutes.

VTY Ports

7. Allow 16 concurrent sessions of remote access.
8. Configure the VTY ports to log input synchronously.
9. Set password to C$$W2
10. Configure idling timeout to 20 minutes and 90 seconds.
11. Save config.

VLAN Configuration

12. Create a VLAN for each of the offices and name them accordingly.
13. Assign access port and trunk port where necessary.

Configure frame encapsulation on a serial interface

Configure MultiPoint Protocol encapsulation and assign IP addresses using the DLCI on the topology.

R1(config)#**int s3/1**
R1(config-if)#**encapsulation frame-relay**
R1(config-if)#**no shut**
R1(config-if)#**int s3/1.1 m**
R1(config-subif)#**IP address 20.10.20.1 255.255.255.0**
R1(config-subif)#frame-relay map IP 20.10.20.2 101 broadcast
R1(config-subif)#frame-relay map IP 20.10.20.3 102 broadcast

R2(config)#**int s3/1**
R2(config-if)#**no shut**
R2(config-if)#en
R2(config-if)#**encapsulation frame-relay**
R2(config)#**int s3/1.1 m**
R2(config-subif)#**IP address 20.10.20.2 255.255.255.0**
R2(config-subif)#frame-relay map IP 20.10.20.3 203 broadcast
R2(config-subif)#frame-relay map IP 20.10.20.1 201 broadcast

R3(config)#**int s3/1**
R3(config-if)#**encapsulation frame-relay**
R3(config-if)#**no shut**
R3(config)#**int s3/1.1 m**
R3(config-subif)#**IP address 20.10.20.3 255.255.255.0**
R3(config-subif)#frame-relay map IP 20.10.20.2 302 broadcast
R3(config-subif)#frame-relay map IP 20.10.20.1 202 broadcast

Network

1. Create a network for each of the offices base on the topology.
2. Assign static IP addresses for the PCs based on their respective network.

Network Routing

3. Use EIGRP to route your network from one destination to another.

Test Verification Result

Ensure that all PCs can ping each other.

OVERVIEW OF A DATA CENTER

A data center is a physical facility that houses an organization's critical IT infrastructure, including servers, storage systems, networking equipment, and other computing resources, designed to centrally store, process, and distribute data and applications, prioritizing security and reliability to ensure continuous operations for business-critical functions; essentially acting as the central hub for managing and accessing an organization's digital information.

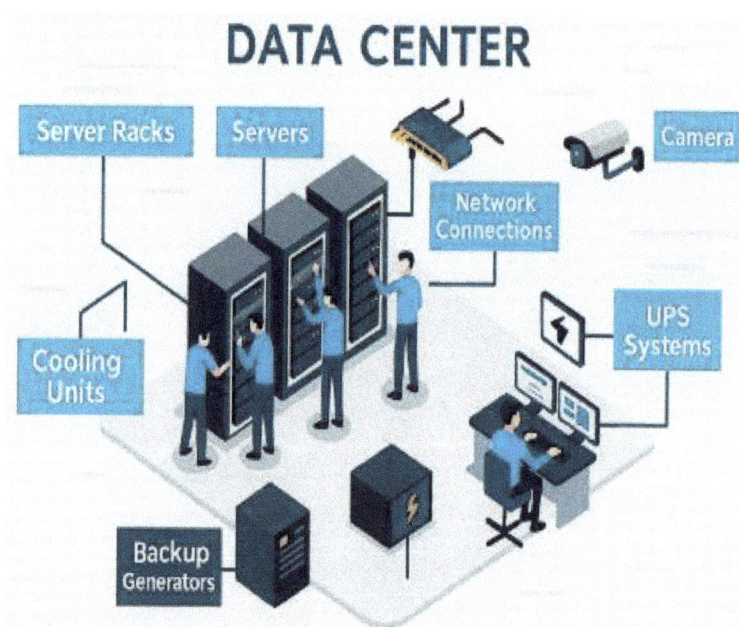

Purpose of a Data Center

To store, process, and distribute data and applications for an organization, enabling access to information from various locations.

Data Center Components

Servers: The primary computing units responsible for running applications and processing data.

Storage systems: Devices used to store large amounts of data.

Network infrastructure: Routers, switches, and firewalls to manage data flow and connectivity.

Cooling systems: Essential to maintain optimal temperatures for equipment functionality.

Power supply: Redundant power sources to ensure uninterrupted operation in case of power outages.

TYPES OF DATA CENTERS

Enterprise Data Centers

These are built, owned, and operated by companies and are optimized for their end users. Most often, they are housed on the corporate campus.

Colocation Data Centers

In colocation ("colo") data centers, a company rents space within a data center owned by others and located off the company's premises. The colocation data center hosts the infrastructure: building, cooling, bandwidth, security, etc., while the company provides and manages the components, including servers, storage, and firewalls.

Cloud Data Centers

In this off-premises form of the data center, data and applications are hosted by a cloud services provider such as Amazon Web Services (AWS), Microsoft (Azure), IBM Cloud, or another public cloud provider.

Why are data centers important to business?

In the world of enterprise IT, data centers are designed to support business applications and activities that include:

- Email and file sharing
- Productivity applications
- Customer relationship management (CRM)

Enterprise resource planning (ERP) and databases

DATA CENTER DESIGN

HIERARCHY DESIGN

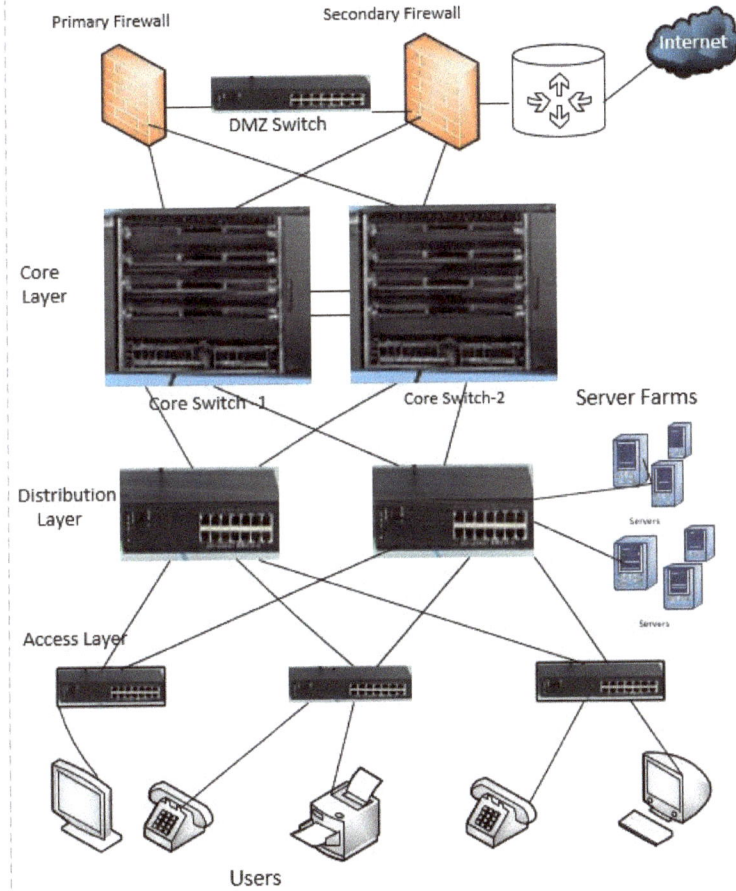

Primary Firewall

Secondary Firewall

Internet

DMZ Switch

Core Layer

Core Switch-1

Core Switch-2

Server Farms

Distribution Layer

Servers

Servers

Access Layer

Users

COLLAPSED DESIGN

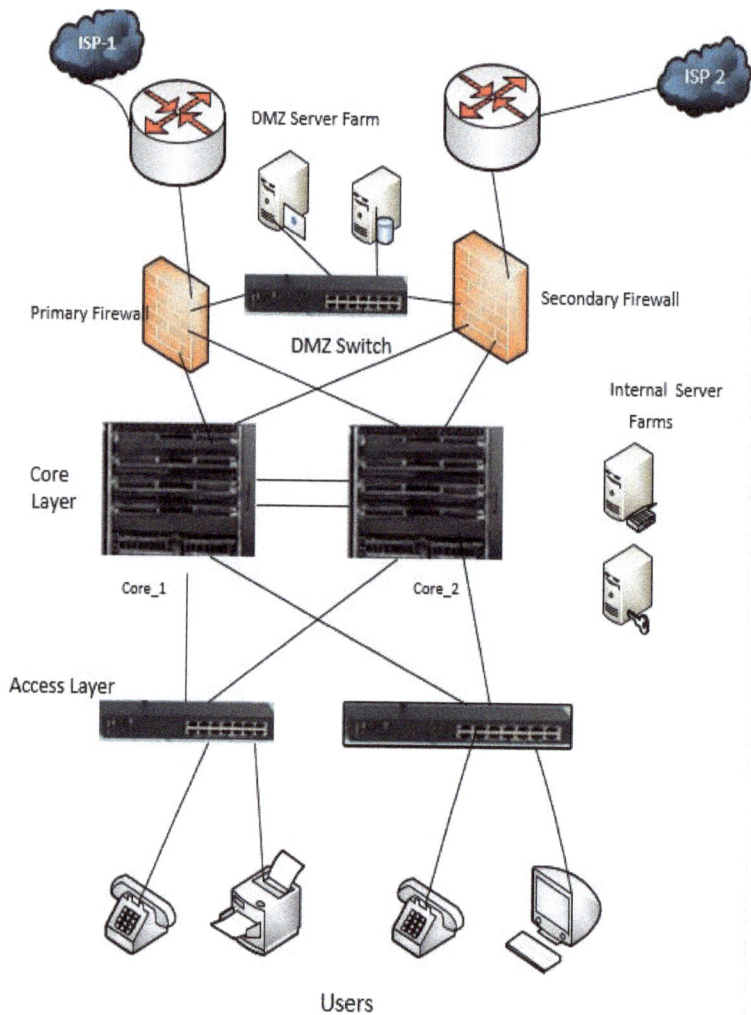

DMZ Server Farm

ISP-1

ISP 2

Primary Firewall

Secondary Firewall

DMZ Switch

Internal Server Farms

Core Layer

Core_1

Core_2

Access Layer

Users

DMZ (NETWORKING)

In computer networks, a DMZ (demilitarized zone), also sometimes known as a *perimeter network* or a *screened subnet*, is a physical or logical subnet that separates an internal Local Area Network (LAN) from other untrusted networks, usually the Internet.

Any service provided to users on the public internet is located in the DMZ. So, they are accessible from the internet, but the rest of the internal LAN remains unreachable. This provides an additional layer of security to the LAN as it restricts the ability of hackers to directly access internal servers and data via the internet.

Some of the common services are DNS, web servers, email servers, and Voice over IP (VoIP) servers.

DMZ NETWORK ARCHITECTURE

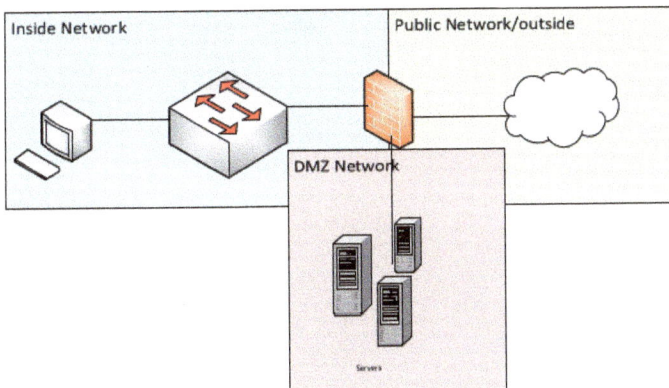

CABLING

Networking cables are networking hardware used to connect one network device to other network devices or to connect two or more computers to share printers, scanners, etc. There are 3 basic types of network cables such as coaxial cable, optical fiber cable, and **Ethernet cables.**

Coaxial Cables

Coaxial cables are commonly used for television, telecom, and other broadband signals. Although in most homes coaxial cables have been installed for transmission of TV signals, new technologies are being used for home coaxial cable for high-speed home networking **applications** (Ethernet over coax).

Ethernet Cables (Copper Cable).

An Ethernet cable is one of the most common forms of network cable used on wired networks. Ethernet cables connect devices within a local area network, like PCs, routers, and switches. E.g., Cat3, 5, 6, 7, and always terminated with RJ 4.

Straight-through or crossover Ethernet Cables

When you connect two devices of different types together, you use a **straight-through cable.** When you connect two devices of the same type together, you use a **crossover cable.**

Ethernet Cables

Roll Over Cable

Rollover cables (also known as **console cables**) are such types of cable exhibiting Null Modem. Basically, these act as a **link or connection between a computer and the router.** These are typically flat and are frequently used for **connecting two devices**. For example, two computers. Keep in mind that rollover cables are used just for the interconnection of any two devices, not for data transfer.

Here is the image of a rollover cable.

Optical Fiber Cable

There are two main types of fiber cables, namely, Multimode and single-mode. Single-mode is used for longer distances, and Multimode is used for shorter distances.

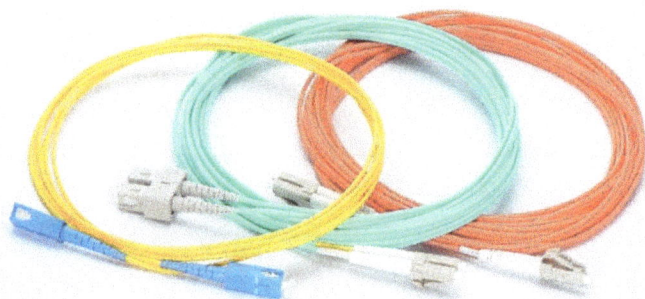

Color	Meaning
Orange	multi-mode optical fiber
Aqua	OM3 or OM4 10 G laser-optimized 50/125 µm multi-mode optical fiber
Erika violet	OM4 multi-mode optical fiber (some vendors)
Grey	Outdated color code for multi-mode optical fiber
Yellow	single-mode optical fiber
Blue	Sometimes used to designate polarization-maintaining optical fiber.

FIBER CABLE CONNECTORS

Fiber Optic Connector Types

LC — Lucent Connectors
- Square-shaped, duplex
- 2.5mm ferrule

SC — Standard Connectors
- Square-shaped, duplex
- 2.5mm-ferrule

ST — ST Connectors
- 2.5mm ferrule
- Spring-loaded, half-turn bayonet-style lock

FC — Ferrule Core Connectors
- Stainless steel screw mechanism
- Ceramic ferrule

FIBER OPTIC TRANSCEIVERS (OPTICS)

SFP and GBIC are the common transceivers for both SM and MM. GBIC stands for Gigabit Interface Converter. SFP is short for Small Form-factor Pluggable. Usually, SFP is considered an upgraded version of the GBIC module. However, GBIC and SFP are equal in performance.

 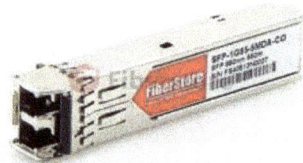

GBIC   SFP

FIBER OPTICS CONNECTORS TO TRANSCEIVER

Fiber-optic cable   Transceiver

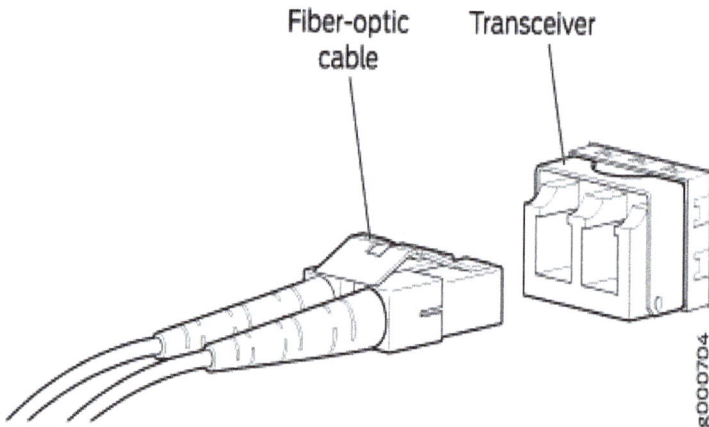

ETHERNET CABLES CONNECTOR

RJ45 is a type of connector commonly used for Ethernet networking.

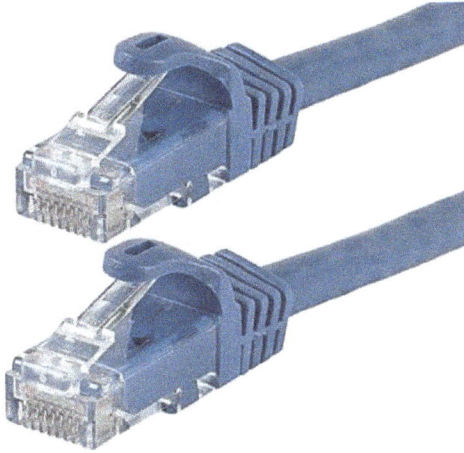

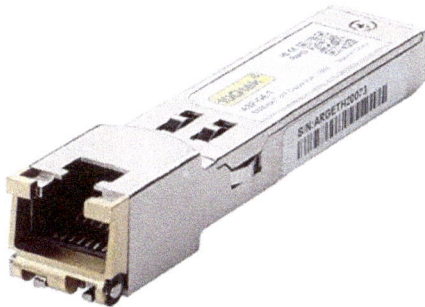

Copper SFP used for copper

MULTIMODE (MM) TRANSCEIVERS

10GBase-SR transceiver

SR stands for Short Range; these transceivers support a link length of 300m over multi-mode fiber and use 850nm lasers. 10GBase-SR is the original multimode optics specification and is still by far the most commonly used.

10GBase-LRM transceiver

LRM means Long Reach Multimode; these transceivers support distances up to 220m over multi-mode fiber and use 1310nm lasers

1000Base SX transceiver

1GBASE-SX transceiver is for multimode fiber cables for less than 550 meters.

SINGLE-MODE (SM) TRANSCEIVERS

10GBase-LR transceiver

LR means Long Reach; these transceivers support distances up to 10km over single-mode fiber and use 1310nm lasers. There is no minimum distance for LR, either, so it is suitable for short connections over single-mode fiber as well.

10GBase-ER transceiver

ER means Extended Reach; the data rate of these transceivers supports distances up to 40km over single-mode fiber and uses 1550nm lasers.

10GBase-ZR transceiver

ZR also stands for Extended Reach, which can transmit 10G data rate and 80km distance over single-mode fiber and use 1550nm lasers.

1GBase LX transceiver

The 1000 base LX transceiver is for single-mode fiber cables up to 10km, and it also supports multimode fiber cables.

Enterprise Cabling Setup

Cabling from wall jack to patch panel to network switch

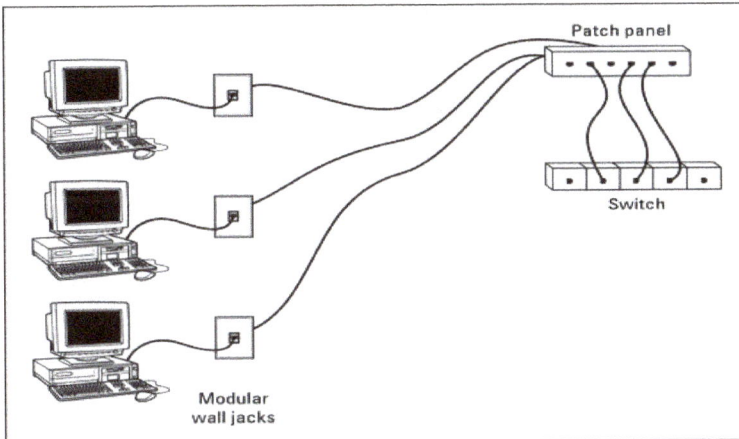

DMARC-DEMARCATION POINT/IDF-
INTERMEDIATE DISTRIBUTION FRAME/MDF-
MAIN DISTRIBUTION FRAME

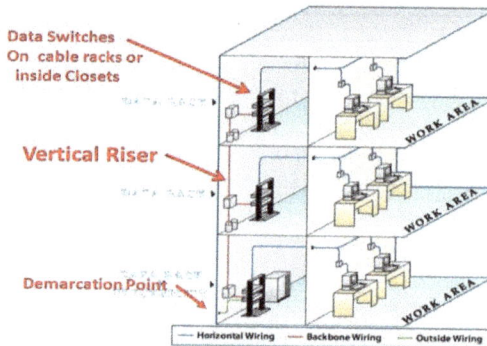

HORIZONTAL & VERTICAL RISER

Data Switches
On cable racks or
inside Closets

Vertical Riser

Demarcation Point

WORK AREA

— Horizontal Wiring   — Backbone Wiring   — Outside Wiring

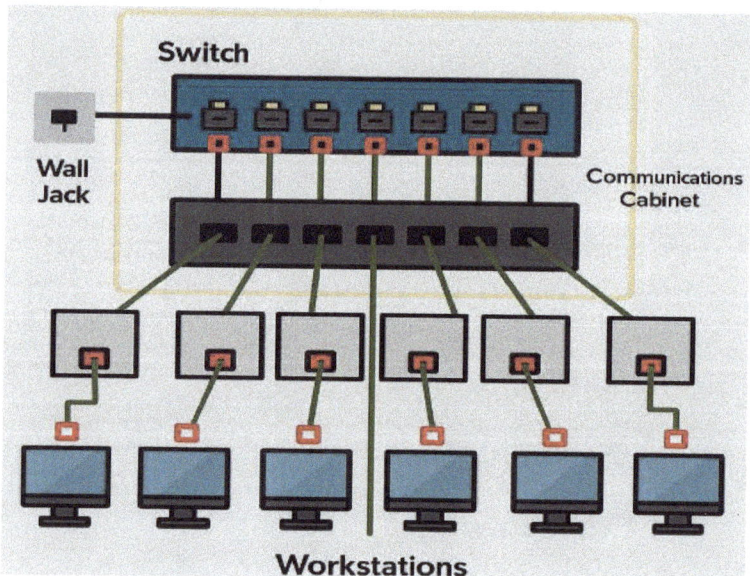

Switch

Wall Jack

Communications Cabinet

Workstations

DATA CLOSET

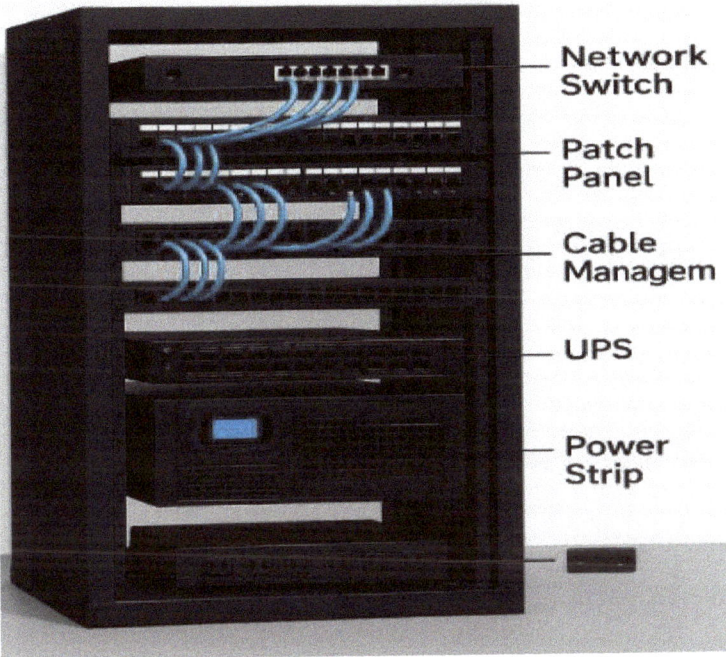

- Network Switch
- Patch Panel
- Cable Managem
- UPS
- Power Strip

WALL JACK

COMPUTER

IDF (DATA CLOSET WITH ACCESS SWITCHES CONNECTED TO USERS)

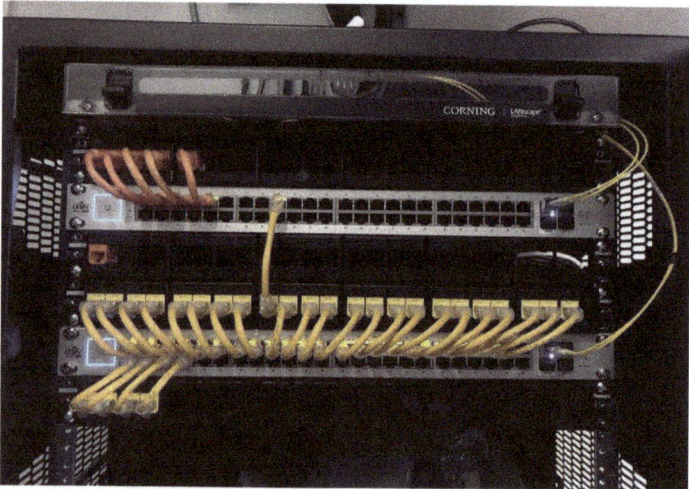

Copper Patch Panel

Fiber Patch Panel

www.networkprofessional.net   training@networkprofessional.net   774-253-62281508-859-0440

Real-life Data closet or IDF with UPS, Switches and fiber patch panels

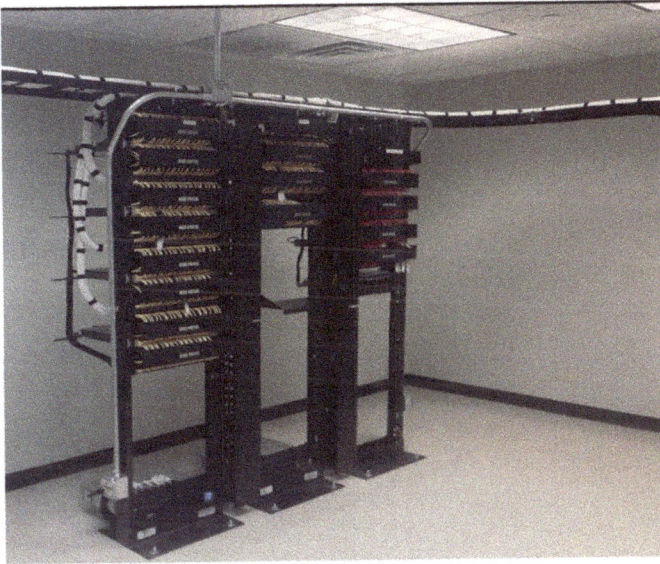

Closet with proper cable management

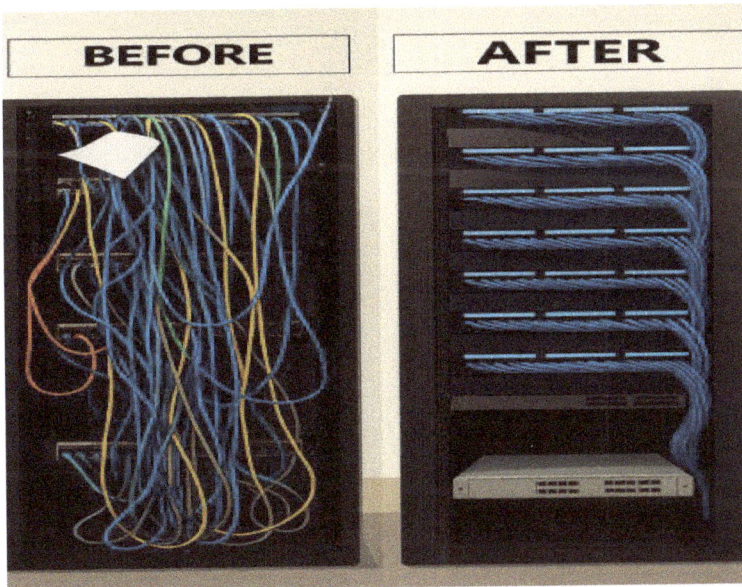

DATA CENTER WITH MULTIPLE RACKS

Cabling from one IDF to MDF or another IDF

MDF Rack

IDF Rack

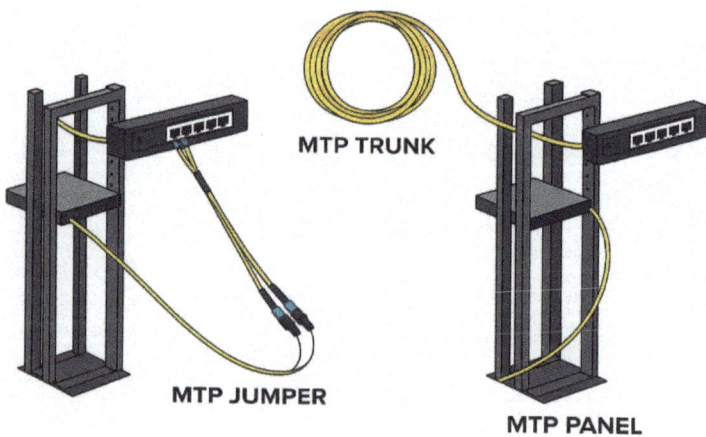

MTP TRUNK

MTP JUMPER

MTP PANEL

Cisco ASA Models

The Cisco ASA – Adaptive Security Appliance

The ASA in Cisco ASA stands for Adaptive Security Appliance.

The Cisco ASA is a security device that combines firewall, antivirus, intrusion prevention, and virtual private network (VPN) capabilities. It provides proactive threat defense that stops attacks before they spread through the network. Therefore, the Cisco ASA firewall is the whole package.

The ASA 5500 series has the following models:

- Cisco ASA 5505
- Cisco ASA 5510
- Cisco ASA 5520
- Cisco ASA 5525-X
- Cisco ASA 5540
- Cisco ASA 5550
- Cisco ASA 5580-20
- Cisco ASA 5580-40

Cisco Core layer Switches

Cisco Catalyst 6500 Core Series Switches

Models-: 6504,6506,6509,6509 Switches EOS| EOS-2025

Cisco Catalyst 6800 Core series Switches

Model: 6807-XL, 6880-x, 6824-X-LE-40G, 6832-X-LE, 6840-X-LE-40G Switch EOS-2025

Cisco Catalyst 9400 Access Series Switches

Model: 9404R, 9407R, 9420R Switches RD 2017

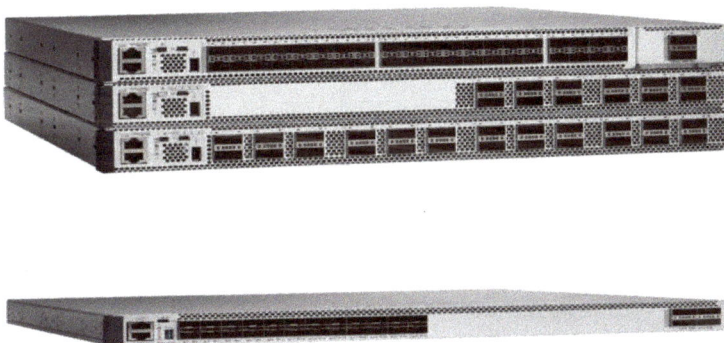

Cisco Catalyst 9500 Core Series Switches

The Cisco Catalyst 9500 Series is the first 100/40-Gbps switch purpose-built for the enterprise campus. It was recently recognized as CRN's 2017 Overall Network Product of the Year.

- Stackable Switches
- mGig
- RD 2017

Cisco Nexus Switches Series

Cisco Nexus switches are a series of modular and fixed-port network switches designed for data centers. They support high-performance networking and are used in various applications, including cloud architecture and high-frequency trading.

Nexus 9000 Series (9k)

Known for its high density of 800G fabrics ideal for next-generation leaf–and-spine network designs

Nexus 7000 series-7k

Offers high performance and scalability with low power consumption

They offer high-density 10, 40, and 100 Gigabit Ethernet with application awareness and performance analytics

EMPTY CHASSIS

Line Card/Network Model/Core Blade

DISTRIBUTION LAYER SWITCHES

The distribution layer is an intermediate layer. These switches bridge the core layer and access layer. The main responsibility of these switches is to ensure the routing of data to the correct devices in the access layer. However, the distribution layer handles maximum data traffic as the data packets are pushed through the core layer to the distribution layer.

For this layer, you can use layer 2 or layer 3 switches. Mostly, layer 2 is used if you want to prevent over-crowding of data packets in transmission links and access devices. This layer plays an important role in directing the data packets to correct addresses, reducing data traffic, and preventing reverse transmission of data through the transmission links.

ACCESS LAYER SWITCHES

The access layer is the most accessed layer of the network hierarchy; switches must be capable of switching and routing data without back-transmission of data. These switches are also can also be layer 2 or 3 switches.

Model: 9400, 9300,9200,3850,3750 switches are stackable switches that can be used for core, distribution, and Access layers depending on the size of the company.

Cisco Catalyst 4500 series Switches

Model: 4503, 4506, 4507 Switch

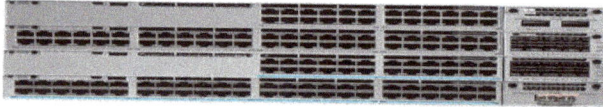

Cisco Catalyst 9300 Series Switches

The Cisco Catalyst 9300 Series, including the new Catalyst 9300X model, supplies up to 1 Tbps of capacity and 90-watt UPOE+ in a stackable switching platform.

Access Layer Switches

Model: 9300,9200,3850,3750 switches are stackable switches that can be used for core, distribution, and access layers depending on the size of the company.

Model: **2960, 3550, and 3650** are all old switches that can be used for the access layer.

CISCO ROUTERS

Common models used in the industries are ASR & ISR routers and Cisco ISR (Integrated Service Routers), typically used as the internet edge for customers with small/medium networks. 2. Cisco ASRs (Aggregation Services Routers) are typically used as an internet edge for enterprise networks and service providers.

Cisco ISR 4000 Series Integrated Services Routers

Model: (4221-RD 2016), (4321, 4331-RD 2014), (4351-RD 2014), (4451-x RD 2013), (4461-RD 2018)

Cisco 2900 Series Integrated Services Routers

Model: 2911, 2951, 2921, EOS| EOS 2022, RD-2009

Cisco 2800 Series Routers

Model; 2851,2821,2811,2801

Other old ISR Models 1800,1900,3800,3900

Cisco ASR 1000 Series Aggregation Services Routers

Model: 1001-X RD 2013, 1002 RD-2013, 1002-HX RD 2016, and 1002-X RD 2012 etc.

Other New ASR Models: 900v, 9001, 9901,9902,9903,9904

WLAN CONTROLLER

A wireless LAN (WLAN) controller, or WLC, is a device that manages and monitors wireless access points. It's a key part of wireless network infrastructure and is usually located in the data center.

What does a WLAN controller do?

- Manages wireless access points in bulk
- Allows devices to connect to the wireless network
- Centralizes wireless network infrastructure
- Allocates bandwidth to access points
- Optimizes network performance
- Limits network downtime
- Fights threats to a business based on user ID and location

Why use a WLAN controller?

- Before WLCs, access points had to handle connections individually, which led to poor connections and unstable data links.
- WLCs help to minimize traffic flow issues and bottlenecks as a wireless network grows larger.
- WLCs simplify the administration of complex wireless networks
- WLCs are essential for organizations with large-scale or distributed Wi-Fi networks

5500 series, 4400 series of WLC

9800 Series of WLC

Models: CW9800M, CW9800H1, CW 9800H2, 9800-L, 9800-CL, 9800-40

FIRST HOP REDUNDANCY PROTOCOLS (FHRP)

First Hop Redundancy Protocol (FHRP) enables redundant routers to share a single virtual IP address as the default gateway, providing seamless failover if the active router fails.

How it works:

Instead of relying on a single router as the default gateway, multiple routers participate in a group, sharing a virtual IP address and virtual MAC address.

Key Features:

Redundancy: Ensures network connectivity even if the primary router fails.

Transparent Failover: End users/devices don't need to be reconfigured or change their default gateway settings during a failover.

Load Sharing: Some FHRP protocols can also distribute traffic among multiple.

Examples of such protocols include:

- **Hot Standby Router Protocol (HSRP) -** Cisco proprietary standard
- **Virtual Router Redundancy Protocol** (VRRP) - an open standard protocol
- **Gateway Load Balancing Protocol** (GLBP) - a more recent proprietary standard from Cisco that permits load balancing as well as redundancy
- **Extreme Standby Router Protocol** (ESRP) - Extreme Networks' proprietary standard with fast failover and also layer 2 protection
- **NetScreen Redundancy Protocol** (NSRP) - a Juniper Networks proprietary router redundancy protocol providing load balancing

Hot Standby Routing Protocol (HSRP)

HSRP is a proprietary protocol from Cisco. HSRP is a routing protocol that provides backup to a router in the event of failure.

In HSRP, only one device is active as a gateway while the other is in the standby state. If the active gateway goes down, then the other standby device takes over.

The device that has high HSRP priority becomes active; by default, all devices have a priority of 100.

HSRP States

When in operation, HSRP devices are configured into one of many states:

- **Active** – This is the state of the device that is actively forwarding traffic.
- **Init or Disabled** – This is the state of a device that is not yet ready or able to participate in HSRP.
- **Standby** – This is the state of a device that is prepared to take over the traffic forwarding duties from the active device. **HSRP routers also go through a number of states before it ends up as an active or standby route.**

- **Initial -** This is the first state when HSRP starts. You'll see this just after you configured HSRP or when the interface just got enabled
- **Listen -** The router knows the virtual IP address and will listen for hello messages from other HSRP routers
- **Speak -** The router will send hello messages and will join the election to see which router will become active or standby.

HSRP PROJECT

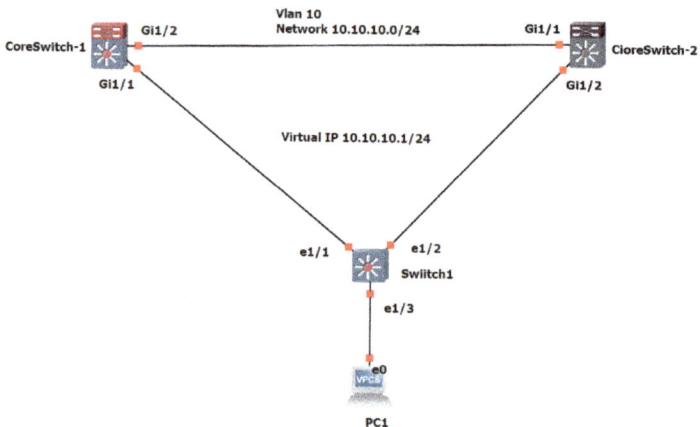

Global Configuration

1. Configure the hostname base on the topology.
2. Disable the DNS lookup feature.
3. Assign R as the Secret password.

Console Port

4. Configure the console port on all devices to log input synchronously.
5. Set password to NPTC
6. Configure the idling timeout to 10 minutes and 30 minutes.

VTY Ports

7. Allow 5 concurrent sessions of remote access.
8. Configure the VTY ports to log input synchronously.
9. Set password to C
10. Configure idling timeout to 10 minutes and 60 seconds.

TYPES OF VLAN

Default VLAN

The **Default VLAN** is simply the VLAN to which all Access Ports are assigned until they are explicitly placed in another VLAN. In the case of Cisco switches (and most other Vendors), the Default VLAN is usually VLAN 1.

Production/Standard VLAN Vs. Extended VLAN

VLANs numbered from 1 to 1001 are considered Standard VLANs, and the VLANs ranging from 1006 to 4094 are considered Extended VLANs.

Secondly, if you create extended VLANs in Version 1 & 2, then your switch must be in transparent mode, as these VLANs cannot be sent in VTP updates.

Extended-range VLANs (**VLANs** 1006 to 4094) are supported only in **VTP version 3**.

Native VLAN

In the case of Cisco (and most vendors), the **Default *Native* VLAN** is VLAN 1. This is to say, if you do not set a Native VLAN explicitly, any *untagged* traffic received on a trunk port is automatically placed in VLAN 1.

VLAN Configuration

1. Configure VLAN 10 and 100 and name it as Data Native VLAN, respectively, on the Core Switch, and let it propagate on the access switch.

Verify your command with the appropriate show command.

Show VLAN-switch.

Trunk Configuration

2. Configure the trunk port base on the topology and use 100 as your native VLAN.

Int G1 /1

Switch trunk native VLAN 100

Switch trunk encapsulation dot1 q

Switch mode trunk

VTP (VLAN TRUNKING PROTOCOL)

VLAN Trunking Protocol (**VTP**) is a Cisco proprietary protocol that carries VLAN information to all connected switches in a VTP domain. When you configure a new VLAN on one VTP server, the VLAN is distributed through all switches in the domain. This reduces the need to configure the same VLAN everywhere. The VTP configuration has a revision number, which will increase when you make a change.

VTP provides the following benefits:

- VLAN configuration consistency across the layer 2 network
- Reduces administration in a switched network
- Dynamic distribution of added VLANs across the network
- Plug-and-play configuration when adding new VLANs

VTP MODES

	VTP Server	VTP Client	VTP Transparent
Create/Modify/Delete VLANs	Yes	No	Only local
Synchronizes itself	Yes	Yes	No
Forwards advertisements	Yes	Yes	Yes

VTP PASSWORD

If you configure a password for VTP, you must configure the password on all switches in the VTP domain. The password must be the same password on all those switches. The VTP password that you configure is translated by an algorithm into a 16-byte word (MD5 value) that is carried in all summary-advertisement VTP packets.

VTP PRUNING

VTP ensures that all switches in the VTP domain are aware of all VLANs. However, there are occasions when VTP can create unnecessary traffic. All switches in the network receive all broadcasts, even in situations in which few users are connected to that VLAN. VTP pruning is a feature that you use in order to eliminate or *prune* this unnecessary traffic.

There are three versions of VTP so far. VTP Version 2 (V2) is not much different than VTP Version 1 (V1). VTP version 3 supports *extended VLANs. SW(Config)VTP version 3*

VTP Version 1 – the transparent switch will only pass updates from the same VTP domain.

VTP Version 2 – the transparent switch will pass updates from any VTP domain.

NOTE: As a best practice, a new switch should be configured as a VTP client in the VTP domain, and its configuration revision number must be set back to zero before being installed into a production network because VTP has a huge security risk... The problem with VTP is that a VTP server is also a VTP client, and a VTP client can overwrite a VTP server if the revision number is higher.

REMEMBER: A VTP client can update other clients and VTP servers in the VTP domain if its revision number is higher.

You can reset the revision number by:

· **Changing the domain name** will reset the revision number.

· **Deleting the VLAN.dat** file on your flash memory will reset the revision number.

INTERVIEW QUESTIONS

- What is VLAN?
- What is the main purpose of VLAN?
- What is native VLAN?
- What are the different VLAN modes?
- What is the difference between VTP Transparent and VTP Client mode?
- Which is the default mode of VTP?
- What is VTP Pruning?
- What are the two benefits of using VTP in a switching environment?
- Which VTP mode is capable of creating only local VLANs and does not synchronize with other switches in the VTP domain?

VLAN TRUNKING PROTOCOL (VTP) CONFIGURATION

1. Configure the VTP domain name and password on both Core switches as follows:

Domain Name – NPTC

Password- secret

Core1

CoreSWITCH1 (config) #VTP domain NPTC

CoreSWITCH1 (config) #VTP mode server

CoreSWITCH1 (config) #VTP password secret

Core2

CoreSWITCH1 (config) #VTP domain NPTC

CoreSWITCH1 (config) #VTP mode server

CoreSWITCH1 (config) #VTP password secret

Verify your command with the appropriate show command

Show VTP status

CoreSWITCH1#show VTP status

Configuration Revision   : 1

Maximum VLANs supported locally: 1005

Number of existing VLANs   : 6

VTP Operating Mode   : Server

VTP Domain Name   : NPTC

VTP Pruning Mode   : Disabled

Show VTP password

CoreSWITCH1#show VTP password

VTP Password: secret

1. Configure the VTP mode of the access switch as a client.

AccessSwitch (config) #VTP mode Client

Verify your command with the appropriate show command

Show VTP status

AccessSwitch#showVTP status

Configuration Revision   : 1

Maximum VLANs supported locally: 1005

Number of existing VLANs   : 6

VTP Operating Mode   : Client

VTP Domain Name   : NPTC

HSRP Configuration

2. Configure the HSRP on the Core switches using group number 10 and make Core_sw2 the standby switch with a priority of 102

HSRP Version Differences

V2 Support IPv6, V1 does not

V2 offers 4095 groups, V1 offers 255

Configuration Guide for Version 2

Interface VLAN 10

hsrp version 2

HSRP Configuration Guide

Core_SW1 (config)# **int VLAN** 10

IP address 10.10.10.2 255.255.255.0

standby 10 IP 10.10.10.1

standby 10 priority 102

standby 10 preempt

Core_SW2 (config)# **int VLAN** 10

IP address 10.10.10.3 255.255.255.0

standby 10 IP 10.10.10.1

SVI Configuration

3. Configure the switch virtual interface (SVI) on the Access_Switch using VLAN 10 as management

Access_switch (config)# **interface VLAN** 10

IP add 10.10.10.4 255.255.255.0

no shut

CoreSWITCH2#show standby bri

P indicates configured to preempt.

|

Interface	Grp	Pri	P	State	Active	Standby	Virtual IP
Vl10	10	100		Standby	10.10.10.2	local	10.**10.10.1**

Assignment IP address for the PC

1. Assign Static IP of 10.10.10.10 SM 255.255.255.0 GW 10.10.10.1

Verify if the PC can ping both core switch
PC1>

PC1>ping 10.10.10.2
84 bytes from 10.10.10.2 icmp_seq=1 ttl=255 time=21.002 ms
84 bytes from 10.10.10.2 icmp_seq=2 ttl=255 time=51.005 ms
84 bytes from 10.10.10.2 icmp_seq=3 ttl=255 time=41.004 ms

PC1>ping 10.10.10.3
84 bytes from 10.10.10.3 icmp_seq=3 ttl=255 time=67.007 ms
84 bytes from 10.10.10.3 icmp_seq=4 ttl=255 time=46.004 ms

Disconnect the Active router and verify your continuous ping

PC1>ping 10.10.10.1 -t
84 bytes from 10.10.10.1 icmp_seq=2 ttl=255 time=25.002 ms
84 bytes from 10.10.10.1 icmp_seq=3 ttl=255 time=28.003 ms

HSRP PROJECT WITH ACCESS_SW IN CLIENT MODE

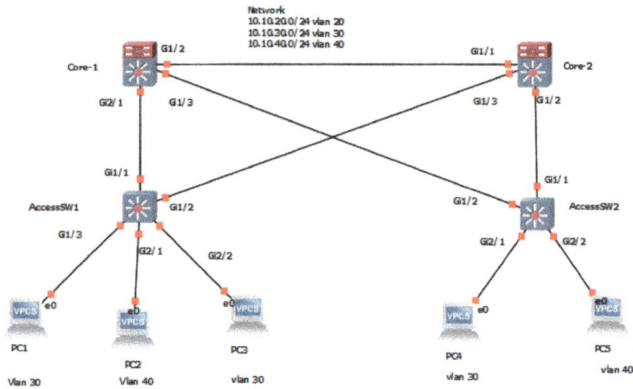

Network
10.10.20.0/24 vlan 20
10.10.30.0/24 vlan 30
10.10.40.0/24 vlan 40

Global Configuration

1. Configure the hostname base on the topology.
2. Disable the DNS lookup feature.
3. Assign Keep it as the Secret password.

Console Port

4. Configure the console port on all devices to log input synchronously.
5. Set password to NPTC
6. Configure the idling timeout to 40 minutes and 60 seconds.

VTY Ports

7. Allow 5 concurrent sessions of remote access.
8. Configure the VTY ports to log input synchronously.
9. Set password to Dat
10. Configure idling timeout to 10 minutes and 60 seconds.
11. Save config.

VLAN Configuration

12. Configure the VLAN base on the topology for both core switches.

Verify your command with the appropriate show command.

Trunk Port Configuration

13. Configure the trunk port and allow VLAN 20, 30, and 40 on the access switch.

Allowed VLAN trunk Guide

Core_SW1 (config)#int G2/1

Core_SW1 (config-if)#switchport trunk encapsulation dot1q

Core_SW1 (config-if)#switchport trunk allowed VLAN **1,20,30,40,1002-1005**

Core_SW1 (config-if)#switchport mode trunk

NB: Always make sure both connected sides on the switch have the same number of VLANs allowed.

VTP Configuration

14. Configure the VTP mode of the access switch as Client.
15. Configure the VTP domain name and password on both the Core switches as follows:

Domain Name – NPTC

Password- secret

Verify your command with the appropriate show command.

HSRP Configuration

16. Configure the HSRP on the Core switches using different group numbers and make Core_sw2 the standby switch with a priority of 102.

HSRP Configuration Guide

Core_SW1 (config)# **int VLAN 20**

#description VLAN 20

 # IP address 10.10.20.2 255.255.255.0

standby 20 IP 10.10.20.1

standby 20 priority 102

standby 20 preempt

Core_SW2 (config)# **int VLAN 20**

#description VLAN 20

IP address 10.10.20.3 255.255.255.0
 # standby 20 IP 10.10.20.1

Core_SW1 (config)# int VLAN 30
#description VLAN 30
IP address 10.10.30.2 255.255.255.0
 # standby 30 IP 10.10.30.1
 # standby 30 priority 102
 # standby 30 preempt
Core_SW2 (config)# int VLAN 30
 # description VLAN 30
 # IP address 10.10.30.3 255.255.255.0
 # standby 30 IP 10.10.30.1

Core_SW1 (config)# int VLAN 40
description VLAN 40
IP address 10.10.40.2 255.255.255.0
 # standby 40 IP 10.10.40.1
 # standby 40 priority 102
 # standby 40 preempt
Core_SW2 (config)# int VLAN 40
 # description VLAN 40
IP address 10.10.40.3 255.255.255.0
 # standby 40 IP 10.10.40.1

1. Use VLAN 20 as management VLAN.

Access_SW1 (config)# interface VLAN 20

IP address 10.10.20.4 255.255.255.0

Access_SW2 (config)# interface VLAN 20

IP address 10.10.20.5 255.255.255.0

VERIFY YOUR COMMAND WITH THE APPROPRIATE SHOW COMMAND.

IP Routing

IP routing is the process of transporting data from source to destination on a determined path across two or more networks. **IP routing enables** two or more devices on different TCP/**IP** networks to connect with each other. **IP routing** provides the path for reaching the destination device.

2. Enable IP routing on the two Core switches.

IP Routing Configuration Guide

Core_SW1 (config)# IP routing

Core_SW2 (config)# IP routing

Access Port Configuration

3. Configure all the access ports.

IP ADDRESS Assignment

4. Assign Static IP to all the PCs.
Verify if the PC can ping each other and the virtual IP

INTERVIEW QUESTIONS for HSRP

- **Ques.** What do you mean by HSRP (Hot standby Router Protocol), or what is the use of HSRP?
- **Ans.** HSRP is used to provide default gateway redundancy
- **Ques.** What are the default HSRP hello and hold-down timers?
- **Ans.** Default Hello timer – 3 sec and Hold down timer – 10 sec.
- **Ques.** What is the default group number for HSRP?
- **Ans.** Default Group number: 0
- **Ques.** What is the difference between HSRP version 1 and HSRP version 2?
- **Ans.**
- HSRP version 1 supports 256 groups ranging from 0 to 255, and HSRP version 2 supports 4096 groups ranging from 0 to 4095.
- HSRP version 2 allows support for IPV6, whereas HSRP version 1 does not support.

Ques. How many states are present in HSRP? **Ans.** 6 states are present in HSRP.

- Init or Disabled
- Learn
- Listen
- Speak
- Standby
- active

Load-Balancing with HSRP

You want to load-balance your traffic between two (or more) HSRP routers/Core Switches. You can configure HSRP so that both routers are always in use if they are available. This allows you to use your network resources more efficiently, but it is slightly more complicated to configure.

Configure the first router as follows, with two HSRP groups:

Router1#**configure terminal**

Router1(config)#**int VLAN 10**
Router1(config-if)#**IP address 10.10.10.3 255.255.255.0**
Router1(config-if)#**standby 1 IP 10.10.10.1**
Router1(config-if)#**standby 1 priority 120**
Router1(config-if)#**standby 1 preempt**
Router1(config-if)#**standby 2 IP 10.10.10.2**
Router1(config-if)#**standby 2 priority 110**
Router1(config-if)#**standby 2 preempt**
Router1(config-if)#**exit**
Router1(config)#**end**
Router1#

Then, on the second router, you create the same two HSRP groups but change the priority levels from those of the first router so that Router1 is active for Group 1 and Router2 is active for Group 2.

Router2#**configure terminal**
Router2(config)#**int VLAN 10**
Router2(config-if)#**IP address 10.10.10.4 255.255.255.0**
Router2(config-if)#**standby 1 IP 10.10.10.1**
Router2(config-if)#**standby 1 priority 110**
Router2(config-if)#**standby 1 preempt**
Router2(config-if)#**standby 2 IP 10.10.10.2**
Router2(config-if)#**standby 2 priority 120**
Router2(config-if)#**standby 2 preemp**

VRRP (Virtual Router Redundancy Protocol)

VRRP, or virtual router redundancy protocol, provides router or switch interface failover and failback facility for seamless operation of a network. If your network is mixed with both Cisco and non-Cisco devices, then it is necessary to use VRRP because HSRP only works with Cisco devices. **Preemption is also enabled by default.**

Show Command (VRRP)

Show VRRP

Show VRRP brief

VRRP PROJECT (ACCESS_SW IN CLIENT MODE)

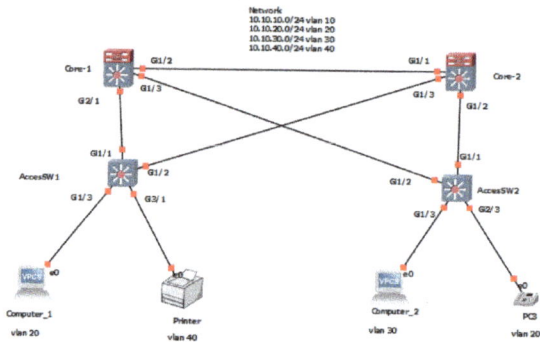

Global Configuration

1- Configure the hostname base on the topology.
2- Disable the DNS lookup feature.
3- Assign Rug@ as the Secret password.

Console Port

4- Configure the console port on all devices to log input synchronously.
5- Set password to N&ptc
6- Configure the idling timeout to 10 minutes and 30 minutes

VTY Ports

7- Allow 5 concurrent sessions of remote access
8- Configure the VTY ports to log input synchronously
9- Set password to Cisc@
10- Configure idling timeout to 10 minutes and 60 seconds

VLAN Configuration

11- Configure VLAN 10,20,30,40, and name it Manangement_VLAN, Finance, Administration, and Engineering on the Core Switch, and let it propagate on the access switch

Verify your command with the appropriate show command

Show VLAN-switch

Trunk Configuration

12- Configure the trunk between the core Switches with no restrictions
13- Configure the trunk and allow only VLAN 10, 20, and 40 on Access_SW1
14. Configure the trunk and allow only VLAN10, 20, and 30 on Access_SW2

VLAN Trunking Protocol (VTP) Configuration

15. Configure the VTP domain name and password on both Core switches as follows.
Domain Name – nptc

Password- secretme

Core1

Core_SW1 (config) #VTP domain nptc

Core_SW1 (config) #VTP password secretme

Core2

Core_SW2 (config) #VTP domain nptc

Core_SW2 (config) #VTP password secretme

Verify your configuration with the appropriate show command

Show VTP status

Show VTP password

16. Configure the VTP mode of the access switches as the Client

AccessSwitch (config) #VTP mode Client

Verify your command with the appropriate show command

Show VTP status

SVI Configuration

17. Configure the switch virtual interface (SVI) on all the Switches and use VLAN 10 as the management VLAN

VRRP Configuration

18. Configure the VRRP on the core switches using different group numbers for all the interfaces and make Core_Switch1 the Master switch

VRRP Configuration Guide

Core_SW1 (config)# int VLAN 10
#description ManagementVLAN
ip address 10.10.10.2 255.255.255.0
VRRP 10 ip 10.10.10.1
VRRP 10 priority 105

Core_SW2 (config)# int VLAN 10
#description ManagementVLAN
#ip address 10.10.10.3 255.255.255.0
VRRP 10 ip 10.10.10.1

Core_SW1 (config)# int VLAN 20
#description Finance
#ip address 10.10.20.2 255.255.255.0
VRRP 20 ip 10.10.20.1
VRRP 20 priority 105

Core_SW2 (config)# int VLAN 20
#description Finance
#ip address 10.10.20.3 255.255.255.0
VRRP 20 ip 10.10.20.1

Core_SW1 (config)# int VLAN 30
#description Administrative
#ip address 10.10.30.2 255.255.255.0

VRRP 30 ip 10.10.30.1
VRRP 30 priority 105
Core_SW2 (config)# int VLAN 30
#description Administrative
#ip address 10.10.30.3 255.255.255.0
VRRP 30 ip 10.10.30.1

DCHP

19. Point the Network 10.0.40.0 to a DHCP Server of 10.51.90.70

Core_SW1 (config)# **interface VLAN 40**

  #description Engineering

  # ip address 10.10.40.2 255.255.255.0

  # ip helper-address 10.51.90.70

  # VRRP 40 ip 10.10.40.1

  #VRRP 40 priority 105

Core_SW2 (config)# **interface VLAN 40**

  # ip address 10.10.40.3 255.255.255.0

  # ip helper-address 10.51.90.70

  # VRRP 40 ip 10.10.40.1

Verify your config with the appropriate show command

IP Routing

20. Enable IP routing on the two Core switches.

Access Port Configuration

21. Assign VLAN 20 port e1/3 on Access_SW1 and set port to 10 speed and full duplex

Access_SW1 (config)#**int g1/3**

  #switchport access VLAN 20

  # switch mode access

  # spanning-tree portfast

  #speed 10

  #duplex full

Verify your Config by show run int g3/1

22. Configure VLAN 40 port e3/1 on Access_SW1 and set port to 10 speed and full duplex

Access_SW1 (config)#**int g3/1**
      #switchport access VLAN 40
      # switch mode access
      # spanning-tree portfast
      # no negotiation auto
      #speed 10
      #duplex full

Verify your Config by show run int g3/1

23. Assign VLAN 30 port e1/3 on Access_SW2 and set the port to Auto

Access_SW2 (config)#**int g1/3**
      #switchport access VLAN 30
      # switch mode access
      # spanning-tree portfast
      # no negotiation auto
      # no speed 100
      #no duplex full

Verify your Config by show run int g1/3

24. VLAN 20 on port e2/3 of Access_SW2 and set the port to auto

Access_SW2 (config)#**int g2/3**
      #switchport access VLAN 20
      # switch mode access
      # spanning-tree portfast
      # no negotiation auto
      # no speed 100
      #no duplex full

Ensure that all connected devices can ping each other

INTERVIEW PREP QUESTIONS for VRRP

Ques. What do you mean by VRRP (Virtual Router Redundancy Protocol), or what is the use of VRRP?

Ans. VRRP is used to provide default gateway redundancy.

Ques. What are the default VRRP hello and hold-down timers?

Ans. Default Hello timer – 1 sec and hold down timer – 3 sec.

Ques. What are the different roles assigned to the routers in VRRP?

Ans: Master Router, the router that forwards the traffic.

Backup Router: The router that is a backup to the Master Router.

Ques: Is it possible to use a real interface IP address as a virtual address in VRRP?

Ans: Yes

Gateway Load Balancing Protocol (GLBP)

Gateway Load Balancing Protocol (GLBP) protects data traffic from a failed device or circuit, like Hot Standby Router Protocol (HSRP) and Virtual Router Redundancy Protocol (VRRP), while allowing packet load sharing between groups of redundant devices.

You can specify three different types of **load balancing in GLBP** using the following command:

Router(config-if)# glbp<Group no>load balancing round robin / Host-dependent / Weighted

GLBP features:

- **Load Sharing:** You can configure the GLBP in such a way that traffic from LAN clients can be shared by multiple routers, thereby sharing the traffic load more equitably among available routers. The load sharing available is:
  - **Host-dependent:** Specifies a load balancing method based on the MAC address of a host where the same forwarder is always used for a particular host while the number of GLBP group members remains unchanged.
  - **Round-robin:** Specifies a load balancing method where each virtual forwarder, in turn, is included in address resolution replies for the virtual IP address. This method is the **default.**
  - **Weighted:** Specifies a load balancing method that is dependent.

GLBP components:

- **Active Virtual Gateway (AVG):** One virtual gateway within a GLBP group is elected as the active virtual gateway and is responsible for the operation of the protocol. This router has the highest priority value or the highest IP address in the group if there is no highest priority. The AVG answers all ARP requests for the virtual router address. Which MAC address it returns depends on which load-balancing algorithm it is configured to use.
- **Active Virtual Forwarder (AVF):** One virtual forwarder within a GLBP group is elected as the active virtual forwarder for a specified virtual MAC address and is

responsible for forwarding packets sent to that MAC address. Multiple active virtual forwarders can exist for each GLBP group.

GLBP PROJECT (ACCESS_SW WITH TRANSPARENT)

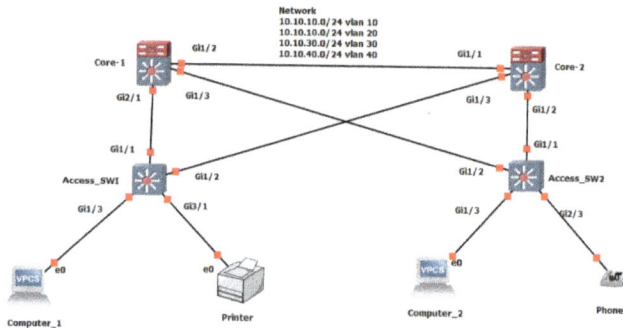

Global Configuration

1. Configure the hostname base on the topology.
2. Disable the DNS lookup feature.
3. Assign R as the Secret password.

Console Port

4. Configure the console port on all devices to log input synchronously.
5. Set password to NPTC.
6. Configure the idling timeout to 10 minutes and 30 minutes.

VTY Ports

7. Allow 5 concurrent sessions of remote access.
8. Configure the VTY ports to log input synchronously.
9. Set password to C.
10. Configure idling timeout to 10 minutes and 60 seconds.

VLAN Configuration

11. Configure all the VLANs on the topology and name them as follows

VLAN 10 Management.
VLAN 20 Printer
VLAN 30 Data for Computers
VLAN 40 Voice for Phones

Verify your command with the appropriate show command

Trunk Configuration

12. Configure the trunk port base on the topology.

VLAN Trunking Protocol (VTP) Configuration

13. Configure the VTP mode of the access switch as transparent.
14. Configure the VTP domain name and password on both Core switches as follows.

Domain Name – NPTC

Password- secret

SVI Configuration

15. Configure the switch virtual interface (SVI) on all the Switches and make VLAN 10 the management VLAN.

GLBP Configuration

16. Configure the GLBP on the core switches using group 1 and make Core_Switch2 the AVF switch.

Core1 GLBP Configuration Guide

CoreSWITCH1 (config)#**interface VLAN10**
CoreSWITCH1 (config-if)#**ip address 10.10.10.2 255.255.255.0**
CoreSWITCH1 (config-if)#**glbp 1 ip 10.10.10.1**
CoreSWITCH1 (config-if)#**glbp 1 preempt**

CoreSWITCH1 (config-if)#**glbp 1 load-balancing round-robin**
CoreSWITCH1 (config-if)#**glbp 1 priority 150**

Core2 GLBP Configuration Guide

CoreSWITCH2 (config)#**interface VLAN10**
CoreSWITCH2(config-if)#**ip address 10.10.10.3 255.255.255.0**
CoreSWITCH2 (config-if)#**glbp 1 ip 10.10.10.1**
CoreSWITCH2 (config-if)#**glbp 1 load-balancing round-robin**

Verify your config with the appropriate show command
Show run int VLAN 10
Verifying GLBP

Commands	Explaination
Router# show glbp	Displays GLBP information
Router# show glbp brief	Displays a brief status of all GLBP groups
Router# show glbp 1	Displays information about GLBP group 1

Access VLAN

17. Configure your port 3/1 as an access port and the rest as voice ports, and set all the ports to auto.

VOICE VLAN/AUXILIARY VLAN (AUX VLAN)

A Voice VLAN, also known as an Auxiliary VLAN, is a feature on network switches that allows an access port to handle both VoIP phone traffic (tagged) and untagged traffic from a computer or other device connected to the phone's backport.

Usually, IP phones sit next to a computer on the same desk. They require the same UTP cables as computers and also use Ethernet. If we want to connect them to a switch, we have two options.

You could connect the computer and IP phone using two different cables for redundancy purposes:

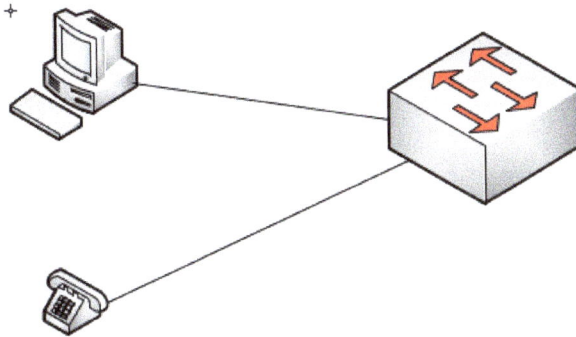

Using one cable for IP phones and a Computer, most IP phones (including Cisco) have a three-port switch inside the IP phone:

- One port connects to the switch.
- One port connects to the computer.
- One (internal) port connects to the phone.

This allows us to connect the IP phone and computer like this:

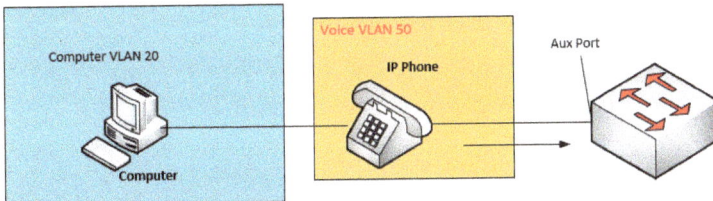

To do the above, we use voice VLAN to separate the data from the computer and IP phone.

The computer will be in a **data VLAN**; the IP phone will be in the **voice VLAN**.

Configuration Guide for Voice/AUX VLAN Port

Access_SW1(config)#**interface GigabitEthernet g1/3**
Access_SW1(config-if)#**switchport mode access**
Access_SW1(config-if)#**switchport access VLAN 10**
Access_SW1(config-if)#**switchport voice VLAN 50**
Access_SW1(config-if)#**span portfast**

Verification

SW1#**show interfaces GigabitEthernet 1/3 switch port**
Name: Gi1/3
Switchport: Enabled
Administrative Mode: static access
Operational Mode: static access
Administrative Trunking Encapsulation: negotiate
Operational Trunking Encapsulation: native
Negotiation of Trunking: Off
Access Mode VLAN: 10 (COMPUTER)
Trunking Native Mode VLAN: 1 (default)
Administrative Native VLAN tagging: enabled
Voice VLAN: 50 (Phone)
Administrative private VLAN host association: none

Above, you can see that we are using VLAN 100 for the computers and VLAN 101 for the IP phones.

IP Routing

1. Enable IP routing on the two Core switches
2. Verify communication among the users

INTERVIEW PREP QUESTIONS For GLBP

- **Ques.** What do you mean by GLBP (Gateway Load Balancing Protocol), or what is the Use of GLBP?
- **Ans.** GLBP is used to provide default gateway redundancy.
- **Ques.** What are the default GLBP hello and hold-down timers?
- **Ans.** Default Hello timer − 3 sec and hold down timer − 10 sec.

- **Ques.** What are the different roles assigned to the routers in GLBP?
- **Ans**: Active Virtual Gateway: the router that forwards the traffic.
- Active Virtual Gateway: The router that is a backup to the Master Router.
- **Ques**: Is it possible to use a real interface IP address as a virtual address in GLBP?
- **Ans**: No.
- What is the main difference between HSRP and VRRP in GLBP?
- **Ans**: GLBP supports load balancing, whereas HSRP and VRRP do not support load balancing.

ETHER CHANNEL PROTOCOL

Ether channel is a technology that lets you bundle multiple physical links into a single logical link. Let's start with an example of a small network:

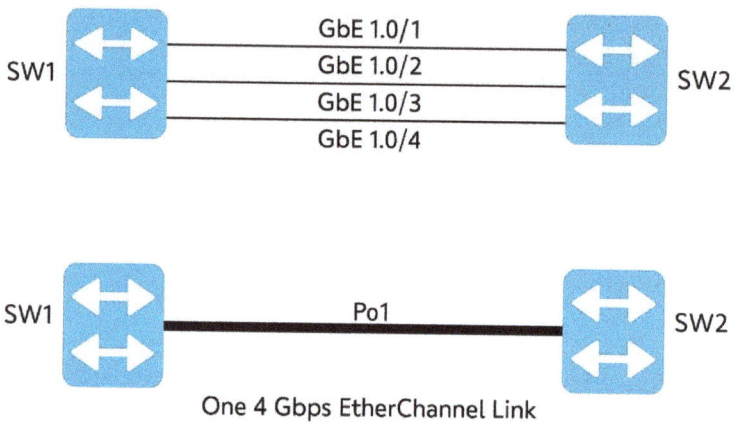

One 4 Gbps EtherChannel Link

Benefits:

Increased Bandwidth: By combining multiple physical links, EtherChannel provides a higher total bandwidth than a single link.

Redundancy: If one of the physical links in the EtherChannel fails, traffic can continue to flow through the remaining links, ensuring network connectivity.

Load Balancing: EtherChannel can distribute traffic across the links in the channel, preventing any single link from becoming overloaded

Use Cases:

EtherChannel is commonly used in high-traffic areas of a network, such as between switches, routers, and servers or in backbone networks.

There's a maximum to the number of links you can use: **8 physical interfaces.**

Types Of EtherChannel

If you want to configure an EtherChannel, there are three protocols you can choose from:

- **PAgP (Port Aggregation Protocol)-** Cisco's proprietary – Dynamic EtherChannel
- **LACP (Link Aggregation Protocol)** – Standards-based - Dynamic EtherChannel
- **Munual Etherchannel ("On")** – Static EtherChannel

Configuration Requirements

If you are going to create an EtherChannel, you need to make sure that all ports have the same configuration:

- The duplex has to be the same.
- Speed has to be the same.
- Same native AND allowed VLANs.
- Same switchport mode (access or trunk).

Port Aggregation Protocol (PAgP) Modes

	Desirable	Auto	On
Desirable	Yes	Yes	No
Auto	Yes	No	No
On	No	No	Yes

Link Aggregation Control Protocol (LACP)

	Active	Passive
Active	Yes	Yes
Passive	Yes	No

EtherChannel "on" mode

EtherChannel "on" mode makes the interface into an EtherChannel without any negotiation protocols like Port Aggregation Protocol (PAgP) or Link Aggregation Control Protocol (LACP). When using an EtherChannel "on" mode, an EtherChannel will be created only when another interface group is in EtherChannel "on" mode.

Etherchanel Project

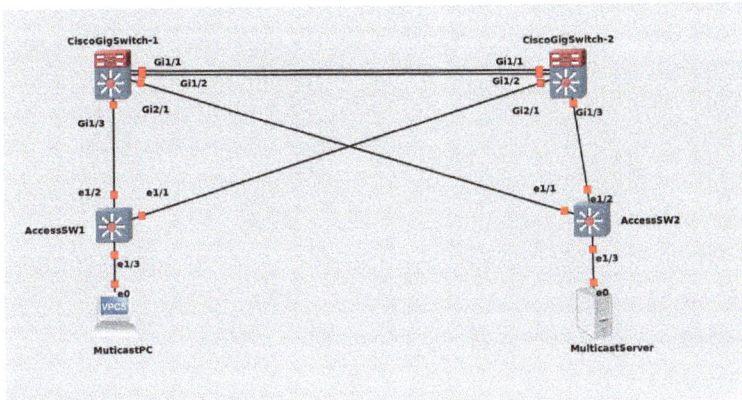

Global Configuration

1. Configure the hostname base on the topology.
2. Disable the DNS lookup feature.
3. Assign Cisc0 as the Secret password.

Console Port

4. Configure the console port on all devices to log input synchronously.
5. Set password to Cisc0
6. Configure the idling timeout to 10 minutes and 30 minutes.

VTY Ports

7. Allow 5 concurrent sessions of remote access.
8. Configure the VTY ports to log input synchronously.
9. Set password to Cisc0
10. Configure idling timeout to 10 minutes and 60 seconds.

VLAN Configuration

11. Configure the below VLAN as follows and allow them to propagate to the access switch.

VLAN 10 – Management VLAN - **10.10.10.0/24**

VLAN 500- MuticastVLAN – **10.10.50.0/24**

MULTICAST AND UNICAST NETWORK

Multicast is the term used to describe communication where a piece of information is sent from one or more points to a set of other points. In this case, there could be one or more senders, and the information is distributed to a set of receivers.

One example of an application that may use multicast is a video server sending out networked TV channels.

Unicast is the term used to describe communication, where a piece of information is sent from one point to another point. In this case, there is just one sender and one receiver.

Broadcast is the term used to describe communication where a piece of information is sent from one point to all other points. In this case, there is just one sender, but the information is sent to all connected receivers.

Broadcast transmission is supported on most LANs (e.g., **Ethernet**) and may be used to send the same message to all computers on the LAN (e.g., the **address resolution protocol (arp)** uses this to send an address resolution query to all computers on a LAN).

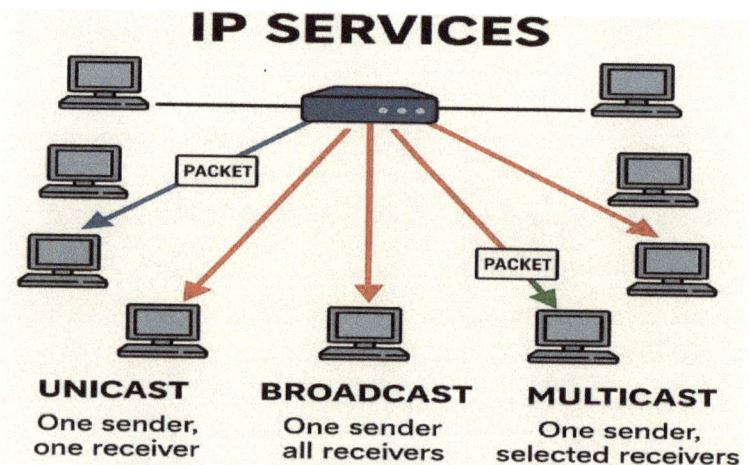

IP SERVICES

UNICAST
One sender, one receiver

BROADCAST
One sender all receivers

MULTICAST
One sender, selected receivers

MULTICAST MODE CONFIGURATION

- PIM Dense mode
- PIM Sparse mode
- PIM Sparse-Dense mode

Here's the key difference between sparse and dense mode:

- Dense mode: **we forward** multicast traffic on all interfaces until a downstream router **requests us to stop forwarding**.
- Sparse mode: **we don't forward** multicast traffic on any interface until a downstream router **requests us to forward it.**

12. Configure a Multicast Network with GLBP using the above ether channel topology

Core 1	Core 1
interface VLAN 500	interface VLAN 500
Description Multicast VLAN	description Multicast VLAN
IP address 10.10.50.2 255.255.255.0	IP address 10.10.50.3 255.255.255.0
glbp 1 ip 10.10.50.1	glbp 1 ip 10.10.50.1
glbp 1 preempt	glbp 1 load-balancing round-robin
glbp 1 load-balancing round-robin	**ip pim sparse-mode**
glbp 1 priority 150	**ip pim sparse-mode**

show command

show ip pim interface

Show run | I ip pim

Sh ip pim neighbor

13. Configure EtherChannel using PAgP with ON mode on Core_SW1 and ON mode on Core_SW2.

Layer 2 EtherChannels (PAgP) Guide

Core_SW1

Core_SW1 # configure terminal

Core_SW1 (config)# interface range G1 /1 -2

Core_SW1 (config-if-range)#Switchport trunk encapsulation dot1 q

Core_SW1 (config-if-range)# switchport mode trunk

Core_SW1 (config-if-range)# channel-group 1 mode on

Core_SW1 # configure terminal.

Core_SW1 (config)# interface port-channel 1

Core_SW1 (config-if)#Switchport trunk encapsulation dot1 q

Core_SW1 (config-if)#Switchport mode trunk

Core_SW2

Core_SW2# configure terminal

Core_SW2(config)# interface range G1 /1 - 2

Core_SW2(config-if-range)# Switchport trunk encapsulation dot1 q

Core_SW1 (config-if-range)# switchport mode trunk

Core_SW2(config-if-range)# channel-group 1 mode on

Core_SW2# configure terminal.

Core_SW2(config)# interface port-channel 1

Core_SW2(config-if)# Switchport trunk encapsulation dot1 q

Core_SW2(config-if)# switchport mode trunk

Ether channel trunk configuration (LACP) Guide (Don't repeat below if you use PAgP)

Core_SW1

Core_SW1 # configure terminal

Core_SW1 (config)# interface range G1 /1-2

Core_SW1 (config-if-range)#Switchport trunk encapsulation dot1 q

Core_SW1 (config-if-range)# switchport mode trunk

Core_SW1 (config-if-range)# channel protocol lacp

Core_SW1 (config-if-range)# channel-group 1 mode Active

Core_SW1 # configure terminal.

Core_SW1 (config)# interface port-channel 1

Core_SW1 (config-if)#**Switchport trunk encapsulation dot1q**
Core_SW1 (config-if)#**Switchport mode trunk**

VLAN Trunking Protocol (VTP) Configuration

1. Configure the VTP domain name and password on both Core switches as follows.
   Domain Name – cisco
   Password- secret

2. Configure the VTP mode of the access switch as the Client

SVI Configuration

3. Configure the switch virtual interface(SVI) on all the Switches

IP Routing

4. Enable IP routing on the two distribution switches

Show command for EtherChannel.

Show int status, Show EtherChannel summary

Layer 3 EtherChannels Project

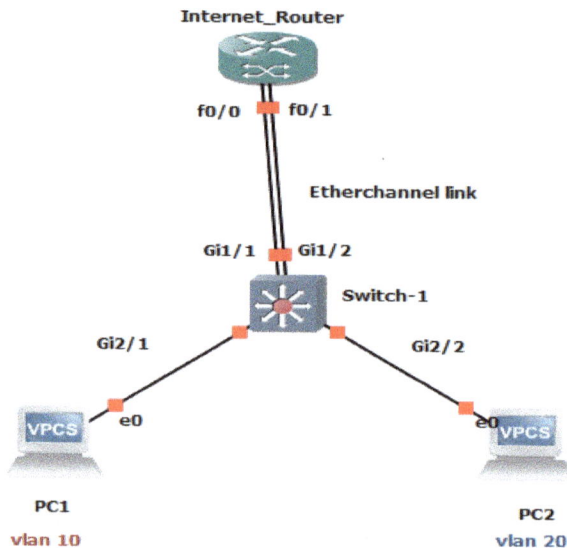

Internet_Router

f0/0   f0/1

Etherchannel link

Gi1/1   Gi1/2

Switch-1

Gi2/1   Gi2/2

e0   e0

PC1
vlan 10

PC2
vlan 20

Router Interface Configuration Guide

Internet_Router (config)# **interface f0/0**
Internet_Router (config-if)# **channel-group 1**
Internet_Router (config-if)# **no shut**

Internet_Router (config)# **interface f0/1**
Internet_Router (config-if)# **channel-group 1**
Internet_Router (config-if)# **no shut**

Internet_Router (config)# **interface port-channel 1**
 Internet_Router (config)# **interface port-channel 1.10**
Internet_Router (config-subif)# **encapsulation dot1Q 10**
Internet_Router   (config-subif)#   **ip   address   10.10.10.1
255.255.255.0**
Internet_Router (config-subif)# **exit**

Internet_Router (config)# **interface port-channel 1.20**
Internet_Router (config-subif)# **encapsulation dot1Q 20**
Internet_Router (config-subif)# **ip address 10.10.11.1 255.255.255.0**
Internet_Router (config-subif)# **exit**

Switch interface Configuration Guide

Switch_1 (config)# **interface range g1/1 - 2**
Switch_1 (config-if)# **channel-group 1 mode on**
Switch_1 (config-if)# **Switch mode trunk**
Switch_1 (config)# **interface port-channel 1**
Switch_1 (config-if)# **switchport mode trunk**

Interview Prep Questions on EtherChannel

Q. What is an EtherChannel?

Ans: It is a method of logical bundling of two or more physical links.

Q) What are the types of EtherChannel?

Ans:

- PAgP (Port Aggregation Protocol)- Cisco's proprietary – Dynamic EtherChannel
- LACP (Link Aggregation Protocol) – Standards-based - Dynamic EtherChannel
- Manual EtherChannel ("On") – Static EtherChannel

Q) What are the advantages of EtherChannel

- We can utilize all the links as STP will not block the link
- Increase speed
- Redundancy (The EtherChannel continues to work till all the links go down)

Q) How many links can we bundle using EtherChannel?

Ans: 8

Q) What are the requirements to configure an EtherChannel between two devices?

- Same Duplex settings
- Same speed
- Same Native and Allowed VLAN
- Same switch mode(access mode or trunk mode)

Q) Why port in the EtherChannel go into a suspended state?

Ans: It goes into a suspended state when the above requirements do not match.

Q) How many ways can you configure the EtherChannel?

Layer2 Ether Channel(No IP address is assigned to the EtherChannel

Layer 3 Ether Channel (IP address is assigned to the EtherChannel)

CISCO SWITCH STACKING TECHNOLOGY.

Cisco switch stacking combines multiple physical switches into a single logical unit, simplifying network management, enhancing redundancy, and enabling scalability. This is achieved by connecting stackable switches through dedicated stacking ports using special cables, forming a unified system that behaves as a single switch.

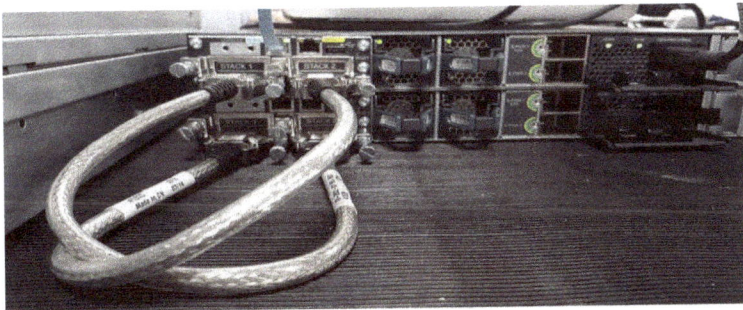

Examples of Switch Models for stacking

- Catalyst 3750 Series:

Supports stacking with up to nine switches connected through StackWise ports.

- Catalyst 3850 Series:

Supports stacking with up to nine switches connected through StackWise-480 ports

- Catalyst 9200 Series:

Supports stacking with up to eight switches connected through StackWise ports.

- Catalyst 9300 Series:

Supports stacking with up to eight switches connected through StackWise-480 ports.

Hardware and Deployment Requirement for Stacking

- Same Vendor and Series:

All switches in a stack must be from the same manufacturer and belong to the same series, as they are designed to work together.

- Stacking Ports/Modules:

The switches must have dedicated stacking ports or modules that allow them to connect to each other.

- Stack Cables:

Use the appropriate stack cables for the specific switch series.

- Physical Space:

Ensure you have enough physical space in the rack or location to accommodate the stacked switches and their cables.

Software Requirement for Stacking

Compatible Software Versions: All switches in the stack must be running compatible software versions.

License Levels: Ensure all switches are running the same or identical license level

Important Considerations:

- Homogeneous Stacking:

Only models of switches can be stacked together.

- Stack Master Election:

One switch is elected as the stack master, which controls the operation of the stack.

Selection of Master Switches

1. **User priority:** we can configure a priority to decide which switch becomes the master.
2. **MAC address**: The switch with the lowest MAC address
3. **Default Configuration**: A switch that already has a configuration will take precedence over switches with no configuration
4. **Hardware/software priority:** The switch with the most extensive feature set has a higher priority than another switch (for example, IP Services vs IP base).
5. **Uptime**: The switch with the longest uptime

Benefits of Stacking:

- **Centralized Management:** Manage all stacked switches through a single IP address.
- **High Availability:** Switch stacking offers redundancy; if the master switch fails, another member takes over.
- **Simplified Scalability:** Easily add more switches to the stack as your network grows.
- **Increased Performance:** Aggregate backplane bandwidth for faster inter-switch communication.

Limitations of Stacking:

- **Hardware Dependency:** Switches in a stack must be of the same model and typically run the same firmware version.
- **Cable Length Restrictions:** Ensure stacking cables meet distance requirements.
- **Master Switch Dependency:** Configuration changes depend on the master switch; a master failure can cause temporary disruption.

VIRTUAL SWITCHING SYSTEM

Cisco's Virtual Switching System (VSS) is a technology that joins two physical Cisco Catalyst switches into one logical switch, thereby joining the two data planes. It's different from stacking switches because you can use regular Ethernet cables rather than stackable cables and modules. The two technologies are otherwise kind of similar in the benefits they offer.

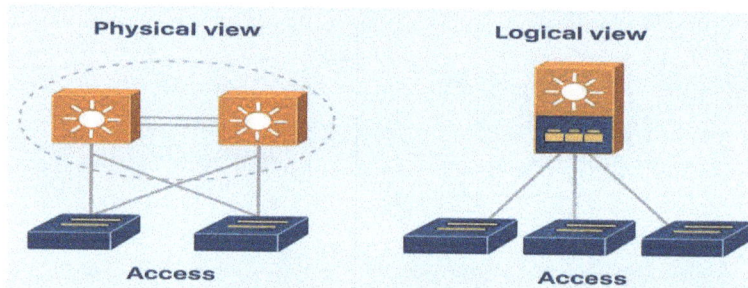

The Virtual Switching System (VSS) allows two Cisco Catalyst 6800 or 4500, and 6500 chassis with higher supervisor engines to bond together so that it is seen as a single virtual switch to the rest of the network. Other devices will see the VSS configured 6500 as a single device, which means it's possible that protocols like spanning-tree will only see a single switch.

Configuration Procedure

In order to bond these two Switches using VSS, we will have to do the following:

- Configure a **virtual switch domain** on both switches and configure one switch as "switch 1" and the other one as "switch 2".
- Configure the **virtual switch links**. [multichassis EtherChannel (MEC)]
- Execute the **conversion** command, which will reboot the switches.

Before you configure anything, verify if the modules are running the same IOS.

WHAT IS THE DIFFERENCE BETWEEN CISCO VSS AND STACKING

At a high level, both sort of accomplish the same goals. VSS is a technology that we see in the 6500, 6800, and 4500 switches. It does not use special cables but establishes a virtual switch link (VSL) between two switches using regular Ethernet cables (Gigabit, Ten Gigabit, etc). VSS is limited to two switches.

Stacking is something we do with 9400, 9300, 9200, 3850, 3750 and 3750x. It uses a special stack cable and is not limited to two switches (some models, e.g., 3570-X, can stack up to 9 members). But The Cisco Catalyst 9300 Series is made up of seven different switch models. Any of the models can be used together in a stack of up to 8 units. This is more of an access layer technology.

VSS Configuration

Step1: Configure a virtual switch domain on both switches with the same ID

Switch 1	Switch 2
conf t	Conf t
switch virtual domain 10	switch virtual domain 10 <-- begins the VSS configuration on the switch
switch 1	switch 2 <-- identifies the switch as switch 1 or 2 of two members
exit	exit

Step 2: Assign a priority number to determine what switch will become active or standby.

SW1-VSS(config-vs-domain)#**switch 1 priority 110**

SW1-VSS(config-vs-domain)#**switch 2 priority 100**

SW2-VSS(config-vs-domain)#**switch 1 priority 110**

SW2-VSS(config-vs-domain)#**switch 2 priority 10**

Step 3: Virtual Switch Link (VSL) to facilitate the communication between two switches.

int range ten1/1 – 2	int range ten1/1 – 2
description VSL1	description VSL2
switchport mode trunk	switchport mode trunk
channel-group 5 mode on	channel-group 5 mode on

Switch 1	Switch 2
int port-channel 5	int port-channel 5
description VSL for VSS	description VSL for VSS
switchport	switchport
switch virtual link 1	switch virtual link 1
no shut	no shut
exit	exit

Step4: Configure the conversion command on both switches

<-- tells the switch to reload and merge with the other VSS member

Switch 1	Switch 2
Switch convert mode virtual	Switch convert mode virtual.

Show Command

Show switch virtual

Show switch virtual link

Show switch virtual role

Show run switch 1

Show run switch 2

Benefits of using VSS for chassis virtualization

- It uses a single database to manage configuration for multiple switches
- It provides a single point of management for improved efficiency.
- Prevent Loops (STP)
- It requires only one gateway per VLAN interface

VIRTUAL PORTCHANNEL

vPC (Virtual Port-Channel), also known as multi-chassis EtherChannel (MEC), is a feature on the Cisco Nexus switches that provides the ability to configure a Port-Channel across multiple switches (i.e., vPC peers).

A virtual port channel (vPC) allows links that are physically connected to two different Cisco Nexus devices to appear as a single port channel by a third device. The third device can be a Cisco Nexus 2000 Series or a switch, server, or any other networking device.

vPC is similar to the Virtual Switch System (VSS) on the Catalyst devices. However, the key difference between vPC and VSS is that VSS creates a single logical switch. This results in a single control plane for both management and configuration purposes. Whereas with vPC each switch is managed and configured independently.

It is important to remember that with vPC both switches are managed independently. This means you will need to create and permit your VLANs on both Nexus switches.

Port-Channels provide 3 key benefits

- **Redundancy** - Should one of the interfaces fail, traffic is sent over the remaining links.
- **Bandwidth** - Increase in bandwidth due to bundling multiple interfaces together. Traffic is then load-balanced across each of the links within the 'bundle.'
- **Spanning Tree** - Port channels are seen as a single switch port by Spanning-Tree protocols.

COMPONENTS OF VPC NETWORK

vPC consists of the following components. The example diagram below shows key vPC components,

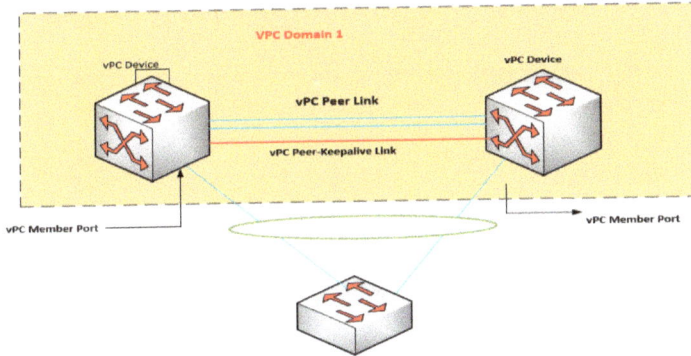

How it works:

- Two Nexus switches are configured as vPC peers.
- Downstream devices (like servers or other switches) can connect to both vPC peers via port channels.
- The vPC technology ensures that traffic is distributed across both physical links, providing redundancy and increased bandwidth.
- One switch is designated as the primary, and the other as the secondary, with the primary handling control plane functions like Spanning Tree Protocol (STP).

Port-Channels provide 3 key benefits.

- **Redundancy** - Should one of the interfaces fail, traffic is sent over the remaining links.
- **Bandwidth** - Increase in bandwidth due to bundling multiple interfaces together. Traffic is then load-balanced across each of the links within the 'bundle.'
- **Spanning Tree** - Port-Channels are seen as a single switch port by Spanning-Tree protocols.

vPC Terminology

- **vPC Peer:** One of the two Nexus switches participating in the vPC configuration.
- **vPC Peer-Link:** The link between the two vPC peers is used for synchronization and control.
- **vPC Peer-Keepalive link:** A link used to monitor the health of the vPC peer switch, sending periodic keepalive messages.
- **vPC Member Port:** An interface that belongs to a vPC.
- **vPC Domain:** The group of vPC peers, peer-link, and all the port channels in the vPC.

What is the functional difference between VSS and VPC in Nexus

These platforms are built for different environments. Nexus is mainly used for data centers and VSS for campus environments. The maximum number of devices you can use for both VPC and VSS is 2.

As far as the difference, VSS has one control plane, vs VPC 2 different ones. With VSS, you eliminate the use of VRRP, HSRP, etc. With VPC, you still have to use one HSRP or VRRP.

Here's a table summarizing the key differences:

Feature	VSS	vPC
Platform	Cisco Catalyst 6800, 6500/4500 series	Cisco Nexus
Control Plane	Single logical node (active/standby)	Two independent, active nodes
Management	Single logical switch	Separate switches
Redundancy	Active/Standby	Active/Active
Layer 3	Supports L3 port-channels	Supports L2 Port-Channels
FHRP	Eliminates the need for FHRP	Still requires FHRP
Port-Channels only LACP.	Supports PAgp and LACP	Support

NEXUS PROJECT WORK

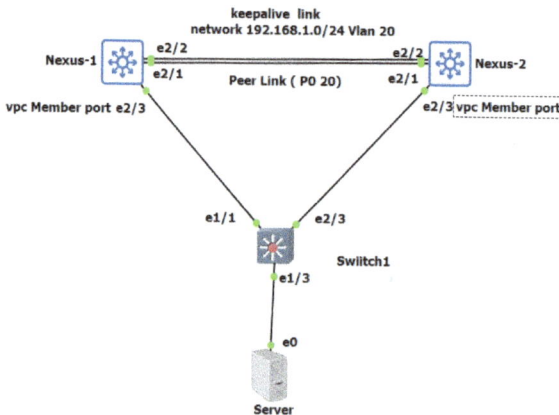

Configuration Guideline

STEP 1: ENABLE THE FEATURES (NB: Apply the same configuration on the second device)

Nexus-1 (config)# **feature vpc**

feature interface-VLAN

feature lacp

Nexus-2 (config)# **feature vpc**

feature interface-VLAN

feature lacp

STEP 2: CREATE VPC VRF ON BOTH SWITCHES (NB: Apply the same configuration on the second device)

Nexus-1 (config)# **vrf context keepalive**

Nexus-2 (config)# **vrf context keepalive**

STEP 3: CREATE VPC DOMAIN ON BOTH SWITCHES (NB: Apply the same configuration on the second device)

Nexus-1(config)# **vpc domain 1**

Nexus-1(Config)#**role priority** 30

Nexus-1(config-vpc-domain)# **peer-keepalive** **destination**
192.168.1.2 source 192.168.1.1 vrf keepalive

Nexus-2(config)# **vpc domain** 1

Nexus-2(Config)#**role priority** 40

Nexus-2(config-vpc-domain)# **peer-keepalive** **destination**
192.168.1.1 source 192.168.1.2 vrf keepalive

N5k-Primary(config-vpc-domain)# **show vpc role**

Step 4: CREATE PEER KEEPALIVE LINK

Nexus-1(config)# **VLAN 30**

Nexus-1(config-VLAN)# **name keepalive**

Nexus-1(config) **interface VLAN30**

Description vPC _Keepalive

vrf member VPC_keepalive

ip address 192.168.1.1/24

Nexus-2(config)# **VLAN 30**

Nexus-2(config-VLAN)# **name keepalive**

Nexus-2(config) **interface VLAN30**

Description vPC_Keepalive

vrf member VPC_keepalive

ip address 192.168.1.2/24

Nexus-1# **show vpc peer-keepalive**

STEP 5: CONFIGURE THE VPC PEER-LINK

Nexus-1 (config)# feature lacp

Nexus-1(config)# interface ethernet 2/1-2

Nexus-1(config-if-range)#description*** VPCPEER LINKS ***

Nexus-1(config-if)# **switchport**

Nexus-1(config-if)# **switchport mode trunk**

Nexus-1(config-if)# **switchport trunk allowed VLAN 20**

Nexus-1(config-if-range)# **channel-group 20 mode active**

Nexus-1(config)# **interface port-channel 20**

Nexus-1(config-if)# **description *** VPC PEER LINKS ***

Nexus-1(config-if)# **switchport mode trunk**

Nexus-1(config-if)# **switchport trunk allowed VLAN 20**

Nexus-1(config-if)# **vpc peer-link**

NB: Apply the same configuration on the second device

Nexus-1# show vpc brief

Nexus-1# **show vpc brief**
Legend:
        (*) - local vPC is down, forwarding via vPC peer-link

vPC domain id   : 1
Peer status   : peer adjacency formed ok
vPC keep-alive status   : peer is alive
Configuration consistency status: success
Per-VLAN consistency status   : success
Type-2 consistency status   : success
vPC role   : primary
Number of vPCs configured   : 0
Peer Gateway   : Disabled
Dual-active excluded VLANs   : -
Graceful Consistency Check   : Enabled

Auto-recovery status   : Disabled
Delay-restore status   : Timer is off.(timeout = 30s)
Delay-restore SVI status   : Timer is off.(timeout = 10s)
Operational Layer3 Peer-router : Disabled

vPC Peer-link status

STEP 7: member port with Access Port Configuration

    interface Ethernet1 /4-5

    description *** ServerNIC1 ***

    switchport access VLAN 10

    speed 1000

    channel-group 10 active

    interface port-channel10

    switchport access VLAN 10

    speed 1000

    vpc 10

N5k-Primary# show vpc | begin vPC status

STEP 8: CONFIGURE Orphan port of DOWNSTREAM DEVICES FOR Access and Trunk

    interface Ethernet1 /1

    description *** ServerNIC1 ***

    switchport access VLAN 10

    spanning-tree port type edge

    no shutdown

interface e3/2

description SW1 connected trunk

switchport

switchport mode trunk

switchport trunk native VLAN 499

switchport trunk allowed VLAN 1,11-12,32,34-35,51-52,60,72-73

spanning-tree guard root

NEXUS VIRTUAL DEVICE CONTEXT (VDC)

The Virtual Device Contexts (VDC) allow a Cisco Nexus switch to be logically segmented into different virtual switches (device contexts). Current software allow only 4 VDCs + admin VDC and 8 + 1

This logical separation provides the following benefits:

- Provides Fault isolation: if any fault occurs in any L2 or L3 process, it does not affect any other processes running on another logical switch.
- Provides management Isolation: each logical switch can be treated as an individual switch and can be managed separately. It can be accessed by a unique individual IP.
- Hardware Isolation: if any hardware resource is allocated to any VDC, it will be part of that VDC till the time admin can reallocate it to another VDC.
- Provides separation of data traffic at the VDC level
- Provide enhanced Security at the VDC level.

Each VDC appears as a unique device and allows for separate Role-Based Access Control Management (RBAC) per VDC. This enables VDCs to be administered by different administrators while still maintaining a rich RBAC capability.

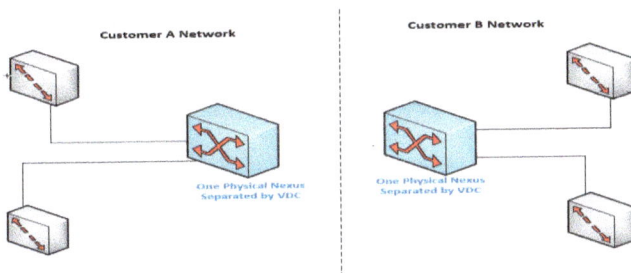

Creating VDCs and assigning ports to the VDC

Step1: Check to ensure how many VDCs are available

show vdc is the command

nexus7000(config-)# do show vdc

vdc_id	vdc_name	state	mac	type
1	nexus7000	active	84:78:ac:59:66:41	Admin

Step2: Creating the VDC

Nexus 7000(config)# vdc VDC-2
Note: Creating VDC, one moment please ...
nexus7000(config-vdc)# do show vdc

vdc_id	vdc_name	state	mac	type
1	nexus7000	active	84:78:ac:59:66:41	Admin
2	VCD-2	active	84:78:ac:59:66:46	Ethernet

Step 3: Then, you can allocate interfaces to the created VDC with the allocate-interface command.

nexus7000(config-VDC)# **allocate interface ethernet 4/5 - 8**

Moving ports will cause all the config associated with them in the source vDC to be removed.

Are you sure you want to move the ports (y/n)? [yes] y

Step 4: Check the port allocations; you can have a look at the show vdc membership module command.

nexus7000(config-VDC)# **do show VDC membership module**

vdc_id: 0vdc_name: Unallocated interfaces:

Ethernet4/17	Ethernet4/18	Ethernet4/19
Ethernet4/20	Ethernet4/25	Ethernet4/26
Ethernet4/27	Ethernet4/28	Ethernet4/29

Ethernet4/30	Ethernet4/31	Ethernet4/32
Ethernet4/33	Ethernet4/34	Ethernet4/35
Ethernet4/36	Ethernet4/37	Ethernet4/38
Ethernet4/39	Ethernet4/40	Ethernet4/41
Ethernet4/42	Ethernet4/43	Ethernet4/44

vdc_id: 6 vdc_name: VDC-2 interfaces:

CLOUD COMPUTING

Cloud computing is the delivery of computing services—including servers, storage, databases, networking, software, analytics, and intelligence—over the internet ("the cloud"). Cloud is used a lot as a marketing buzzword.

Cloud Computing provides an alternative to the on-premises data center. With an on-premises data center, we have to manage everything, such as purchasing and installing hardware, virtualization, installing the operating system and any other required applications, setting up the network, configuring the firewall, and setting up storage for data. After doing all the setup, we become responsible for maintaining it through its entire lifecycle.

But if we choose Cloud Computing, a cloud vendor is responsible for the hardware purchase and maintenance. They also provide a wide variety of software and platforms as a service. We can take any required services on rent. The cloud computing services will be charged based on usage.

Advantages of cloud computing

- **Cost:** It reduces the huge capital expenses of buying hardware and software.
- **Speed:** Resources can be accessed in minutes, typically within a few clicks, giving businesses a lot of flexibility and taking the pressure off capacity planning.
- **Scalability:** We can increase or decrease the requirement of resources according to the business requirements, which means delivering the right amount of IT resources
- **Productivity:** While using cloud computing, we put less operational effort. We do not need to apply patching, as we need to maintain hardware and software. So in this way, the IT team can be more productive and focus on achieving business goals.
- **Reliability:** Backup and recovery of data are less expensive and very fast for business continuity.
- **Security:** Many cloud vendors offer a broad set of policies, technologies, and controls that strengthen our data security.

Types of Cloud Computing/Deployment Models

- **Public Cloud:** The cloud resources that are owned and operated by a third-party cloud service provider (eg AWS, Microsoft Azure, and Google Cloud) are termed public clouds. It delivers computing resources such as servers, software, and storage over the internet.
- **Private Cloud:** The cloud computing resources that are exclusively used inside a single business or organization are termed a private cloud. A private cloud may physically be located on the company's on-site data center or hosted by a third-party service provider.
- **Hybrid Cloud:** It is the combination of public and private clouds, which is bound together by technology that allows data applications to be shared between them. A hybrid cloud provides flexibility and more deployment options to the business.

Types of Cloud Services

1. **Infrastructure as a Service (IaaS):** IaaS provides users with on-demand access to computing resources like servers, storage, and networking. Users are responsible for managing the operating systems, middleware, and applications on top of this infrastructure.
2. **Platform as a Service (PaaS):** PaaS offers a complete cloud-hosted platform for developing, running, and managing applications. Users can use the platform to build and deploy applications without managing the underlying infrastructure.
3. **Software as a Service (SaaS):** SaaS provides access to ready-to-use, cloud-hosted application software. Users can access the software through a web browser or other interface, and the provider manages the underlying infrastructure and software.

Types of Cloud Computing

On Premise		IaaS (Infrastructure as a Service)		PaaS (Platform as a Service)		SaaS (Software as a Service)	
						Applications	
	Applications		Applications		Applications		
	Runtime		Runtime		Runtime		Runtime
Customer Managed	Runtime	Customer Managed	Runtime	Customer Managed	Runtime		Runtime
	Middleware		Middleware		Middleware		Middleware
	OS		OS		OS	Provider Managed	OS
	Virtualization		Virtualization		Virtualization		Virtualization
	Servers		Servers	Provider Managed	Servers		Servers
	Storage	Provider Managed	Storage		Storage		Storage
	Networking		Networking		Networking		Networking

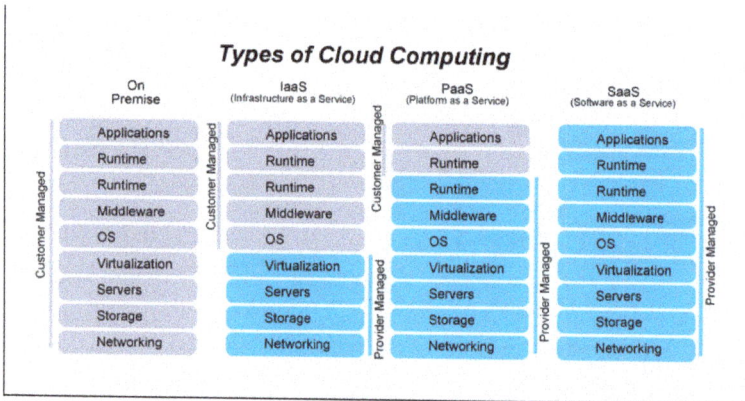

WAN TRAFFIC PATH TO CLOUD SERVICES

The WAN (Wide Area Network) traffic path to cloud services refers to how data travels from an organization's on-premises network to cloud-hosted applications or resources. This path varies depending on the network architecture, cloud connectivity, and deployment model

Direct Internet Access

Using the Internet to connect to the cloud is a common option.

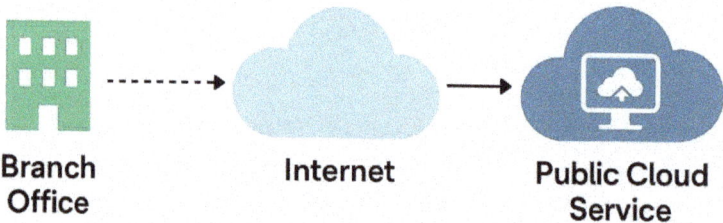

Branch Office　　**Internet**　　**Public Cloud Service**

Above, we see that all virtual machines are located at the cloud provider. The enterprise network doesn't have any servers or virtual machines anymore, only users who require access to the applications that run on the virtual machines.

The advantages of using the Internet as your WAN connection to the cloud are:

- **Cost**: Internet access is cheap compared to private WAN options.
- **Availability**: it's easy to get an Internet connection, and it's available almost everywhere.
- **Migration**: want to switch from one cloud provider to another? All cloud providers are connected to the Internet, so you don't have to switch connections.
- **Mobile users**: If you have a lot of mobile users, then they will be able to access your applications whenever they have an Internet connection.

Some of the disadvantages:

- **Security**: The Internet is a public network, so it's not a very safe place. Attackers might attempt man-in-the-middle attacks to snoop on the traffic between your users and the cloud.
- **Bandwidth**: Depending on the type of applications and the number of users, your Internet connection might not have enough bandwidth for all users to access their applications.
- **QoS (Quality of Service)**: The Internet is best-effort only, and there is no quality of service. If you have any applications that are sensitive to delay and/or packet loss, then you might run into issues.
- **SLA**: most Internet providers don't offer any SLAs (Service Level Agreements) that guarantee a certain bandwidth or availability. If you outsource all or most of your applications to the cloud, you will be very dependent on your Internet connection.

Private WAN

An alternative connection method is the private WAN. This is a dedicated connection from your site to the cloud provider.

Private Dedicated Path

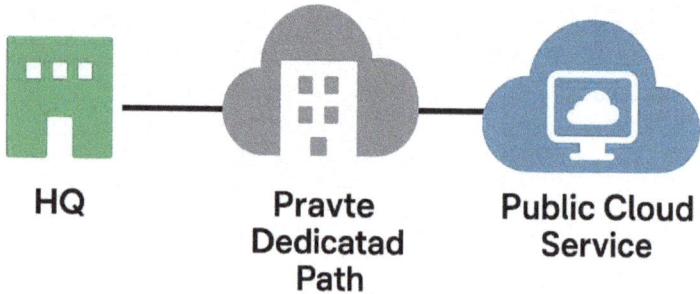

HQ **Pravte Dedicatad Path** **Public Cloud Service**

Advantages:

- **Bandwidth**: Private WAN connections offer a higher bandwidth than most Internet connections.
- **SLA**: does offer service level agreements that guarantee a certain bandwidth and availability.

Disadvantages:

- **Cost**: Private WAN connections cost more than regular Internet connections.
- **Availability**: it takes time to install the new connection.
- **Flexibility**: You are stuck with one cloud provider.
- Here are some examples of private WAN connections:

Microsoft Azure ExpressRoute

A **private, dedicated network connection** between on-premises or colocation environments and Azure datacenters—bypassing the public internet for improved reliability, speed, and security

Amazon AWS Direct Connect

AWS Direct Connect (DX) establishes a private, dedicated network connection between your on-premises network (data center, office, or colocation) and AWS—bypassing the public internet to deliver low-latency, consistent performance. It supports virtual interfaces (VIFs) for accessing AWS public services, VPCs, or transit gateways.

Google Cloud Dedicated Interconnect

Cloud Interconnect provides low-latency, high-availability connections that enable you to reliably transfer data between your networks. Cloud Interconnect offers the following options for extending your network: Cloud Interconnect type. Description. Dedicated Interconnect

Intercloud Exchange

Think of **Intercloud Exchange** as a **multi-cloud switchboard** inside a data center. Rather than setting up separate private links to each cloud provider, you connect **once** to the exchange, and then **virtually peer** with any supported cloud or service provider

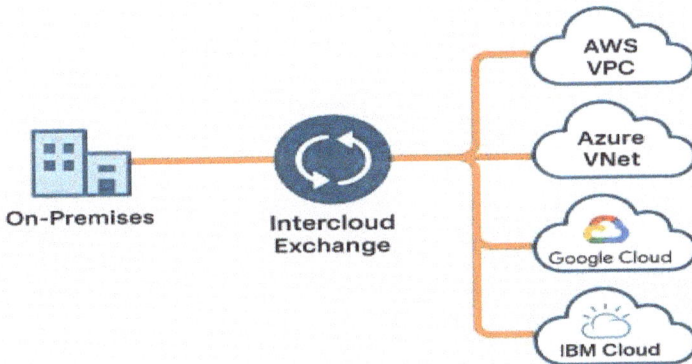

The intercloud exchange can offer you a connection to one or more cloud providers without having to switch your private WAN connection. You get the advantage of a private WAN without being stuck to one cloud provider.

Virtual Network Functions

Virtual Network Functions (VNFs) are software-based implementations of traditional network services—like firewalls, load balancers, routers, and WAN optimizers—that run on standard hardware instead of proprietary appliances.

Most cloud providers offer some basic networking functions. You can choose if your virtual machines have public IP addresses so that you can directly reach them from the Internet or if they use private IP addresses with a router and/or load balancer in front of them. The router and the load balancer that the cloud provider offers, however, have limited options.

A VNF is the virtual version of your favorite router, firewall, or other network devices. Here are two examples:

- Cisco Cloud Services Router 1000V Series: This CSR is a virtual IOS XE router that offers the same features as physical Cisco IOS XE routers.
- Cisco ASAv: This is the virtual version of the Cisco ASA firewall.

You can add them to your cloud network if needed:

This will give you the same networking features at the cloud provider network as those that you use on your own enterprise network.

Physical Data Center Network

What does it look like in a real data center network where we have racks full of servers? There are two common options. Let's take a look at both.

TOR (Top of Rack)

In Top-of-Rack (ToR) network designs, a network switch is placed at the top (or sometimes middle) of each server rack, forming a crucial part of data center network architecture

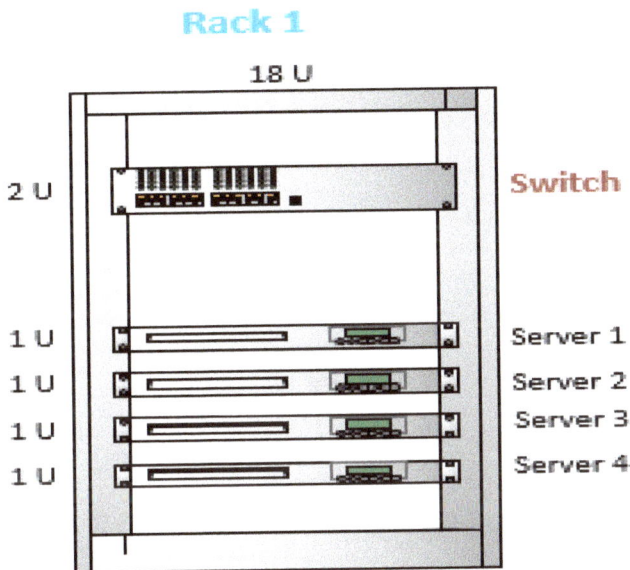

Rack 1

18 U

2 U — Switch

1 U — Server 1
1 U — Server 2
1 U — Server 3
1 U — Server 4

EOR (End of Row)

EOR (End of Row) refers to a network architecture where network switches are positioned in a dedicated cabinet or rack located at either end of a row of server cabinets

With the end-of-row design, there are no switches in the racks, and all servers are directly connected to EoR (End-of-row) switches that are located in a separate rack:

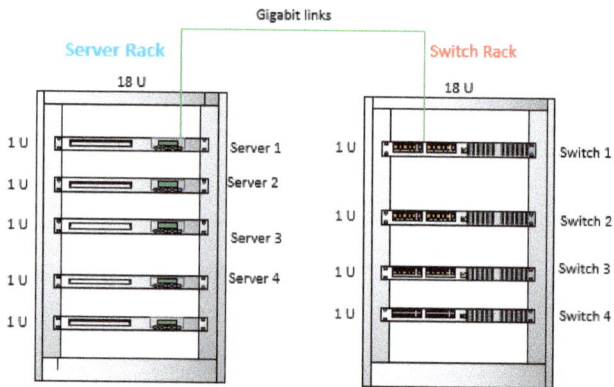

Some of the advantages of this setup are that you don't need as many switches, there are fewer unused switch ports, and overall port utilization is better. One of the disadvantages is that you need a lot of long cabling from your server racks to the racks where the EoR switches are located.

ACCESS CONTROL LIST

A **network access control list** (**ACL**) is a set of rules that determine which users or systems can access specific network resources or devices. ACLs can be configured to allow or deny traffic based on various criteria like IP addresses, protocols, and ports. They are often used in routers and firewalls to control network traffic flow and enhance security by preventing unauthorized access.

How it works:

- ACLs are typically implemented on devices like routers and firewalls.
- When a packet of data enters a network, the router or firewall checks it against the ACL rules.
- If a match is found, the ACL either allows or denies the packet based on the rule's action.
- If no match is found, the packet is typically dropped or handled according to the system's default behavior.

Importance of ALC

- **Security:** ACLs help protect networks by preventing unauthorized access to sensitive data and resources.
- **Traffic control:** They can be used to manage and prioritize network traffic flow.
- **Network segmentation:** ACLs can be used to separate different parts of a network, improving security and efficiency.
- **Policy enforcement:** They ensure that network traffic adheres to established security policies.

TYPES OF ACL

Access Control Lists (ACLs) are broadly categorized into two main types: **standard and extended.**

Standard Access List

These are the simplest types, filtering traffic based solely on the source IP address. They are less complex to configure and require less CPU power, making them suitable for basic network security needs.

Standard-numbered IPv4 ACLs are created by following the global configuration command:

access-list {1-99 | 1300-1999} {permit | deny} *matching-parameters*

Each standard numbered ACL has one or more **access-list** commands with the same number from the 1-99 or 1300-1999 range. You can pick absolutely any number from the allowed range for a standard ACL. Each **access-list** statement also has the **permit** or **deny** keyword to specify the action to be taken when a packet matches the statement. Besides the ACL number and action, you have to specify the source IPv4 address or a range of source IPv4 addresses using a *wildcard mask*.

Extended ACL

Extended ACLs offer a higher degree of control by examining both the source and destination IP addresses, port numbers, and protocols like TCP, UDP, and ICMP. This allows for more specific traffic filtering rules.

Extended ACLs are just like the standard ones, with the exception that protocol and port information can be used, and both the source and destination networks may be defined in the rules. Extended ACLs use designated numbers 100 through 199 and 2000 to 2699. Just like standard ACLs, the subnet mask uses wildcard masks when configuring the subnetwork. Extended ACLs can be configured to match an IP (which includes both TCP and UDP.

What is the difference between standard ACL and extended ACL?

Standard ACL	Extended ACL
Allow filtering based on source address.	Allow filtering based on source and destination addresses, as well as protocol and port number.
Used to block a particular host, network, or subnet.	Used to block particular services.
Standard ACL is implemented close to the destination	Extended ACL is implemented close to the source.
Standard ACL Range->1 – 99 & 1300-1999.	Extended ACL Range->100 – 199 & 2000 – 2699
In Standard ACL, two-way communications will be blocked	In Extended ACL, one-way communication will be blocked
In Standard ACL, all services will be blocked	Extended ACL, a particular service is blocked

ACL PROJECT

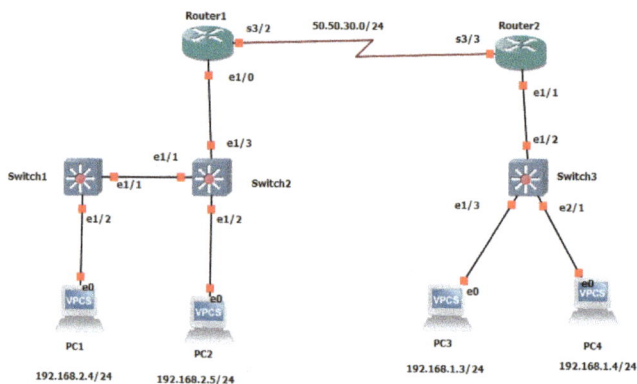

Global Configuration

1. Configure a hostname for all the devices.
2. Disable the DNS lookup feature.
3. Assign R@ng as the Secret password.

Console Port

4. Configure the console port on all devices to log input synchronously.
5. Set password to N
6. Configure the idling timeout to 10 minutes and 40 minutes.

VTY Ports

7. Allow 5 concurrent sessions of remote access.
8. Configure the VTY ports to log input synchronously.
9. Set password to C.
10. Configure idling timeout to 30 minutes and 90 seconds.

VLAN Configuration

11. Create a LAN/WAN for the two offices.
12. Assign access port and trunk port where necessary.

Network

13. Create a network for each of the offices on the topology.
14. Assign static IP addresses for the PCs base on their respective network.

Network Routing

15. Use a Static routing protocol to route your network from one destination to another.

Test Verification Result

Ensure that all PCs can ping each other.

Allow only PC 1 to access both the server and the Printer.

Configuration Guide for Number Standard ACL

R1(config)#access-list 1 ?

deny   Specify packets to reject

permit Specify packets to be forward

remark Access list entry comment

R1(config)#access-list 1 permit 192.168.2.4

R1#show access-lists

Standard IP access list 1

10 permit 192.168.2.4

R1(config)#int e1/0.10

R1(config-subif)#ip access-group 1 in

Test Result

PC1 will allow you to talk to PC3 & PC4, and PC2 will not as shown below:
PC2> ping 192.168.1.3
*192.168.1.1 icmp_seq=1 ttl=255 time=26.003 ms (ICMP type:3, code:13, Communication administratively prohibited)
*192.168.1.1 icmp_seq=2 ttl=255 time=22.002 ms (ICMP type:3, code:13, Communication administratively prohibited)
*192.168.1.1 icmp_seq=3 ttl=255 time=27.003 ms (ICMP type:3, code:13, Communication administratively prohibited)
PC2> ping 192.168.1.4
*192.168.1.1 icmp_seq=1 ttl=255 time=23.003 ms (ICMP type:3, code:13, Communication administratively prohibited)
*192.168.1.1 icmp_seq=2 ttl=255 time=19.002 ms (ICMP type:3, code:13, Communication administratively prohibited)

PC1> ping 192.168.2.3
192.168.2.3 icmp_seq=1 timeout
192.168.2.3 icmp_seq=2 timeout
84 bytes from 192.168.2.3 icmp_seq=3 ttl=62 time=39.004 ms
84 bytes from 192.168.2.3 icmp_seq=4 ttl=62 time=39.004 ms
84 bytes from 192.168.2.3 icmp_seq=5 ttl=62 time=41.005 ms

PC1> ping 192.168.2.4
84 bytes from 192.168.2.4 icmp_seq=3 ttl=62 time=60.006 ms
84 bytes from 192.168.2.4 icmp_seq=4 ttl=62 time=41.005 ms
84 bytes from 192.168.2.4 icmp_seq=5 ttl=62 time=40.004 ms

Name Standard Access List

Name access lists are much like numbered access lists, but with names and the addition of numbers. You can specify what line you wish to place in the ACL. For example, you can have ACL lines 5, 10, 15,20,25,30, and you need to stick an entry between lines without having to remove the entire access list. The new ACL statement will follow a specific line number when in name access-list configuration mode.

Create a Standard name access list and permit only PC2 to access the server and the Printer.

R1 (config)#**ip access-list standard INSIDE_IN**
R1 (config-std-nacl)#**10 permit 192.168.2.5**
R1 (config-std-nacl)#**exit**
R1 (config)#**int e1/0** .10
R1 (config-subif)#**ip access-group INSIDE_IN in**
Test form PC 1 and PC2

Extended ACL

Extended ACLs are just like the standard ones, with the exception that protocol and port information can be used, and both the source and destination networks may be defined in the rules. Extended ACLs use designated numbers 100 through 199 and 2000 to 2699. Just like standard ACLs, the subnet mask uses wildcard masks when configuring the subnetwork. Extended ACLs can be configured to match an IP (which includes both TCP and UDP.

Applying the ACL

Creating ACL is the first step in a two-step packet filtering configuration process. The second step is to apply an ACL to a specific interface. To do so, you must apply the ACL number to the interface and then specify if the ACL should be applied to inbound traffic entering the interface or outbound traffic exiting the interface. Applying an ACL to an interface is the same, no matter if you are using a standard or extended ACL type.

TASK-1

Denies host from 192.168.2.4 to 192.168.1.4

access-list 101 deny ip host 192.168.2.4 host 192.168.1.4

access-list 101 permit ip any any

int s3/2

ip access-group 101 out

TASK-1

Denies telnet traffic from 192.168.1.2 to 192.168.2.2. You should note the use of the **eq** operator and TCP port number 20 to identify telnet traffic. Please keep in mind that we are matching TCP destination ports here.

access-list 101 deny tcp host 192.168.2.2 host 192.168.1.2 eq 23

access-list 101 permit ip any any

int s3/2

ip access-group 101 out

Interview Questions for ACL

Q) What is an Access list?

Ans: Access-List is a method of providing basic-level security.

Q) What is the function of Access-List?

Ans: Access-list is going to filter incoming as well as outgoing traffic on the router interface

Q0 What is the default wildcast Mask for the access list?

Ans: 0.0.0.0.

Q) How many Access lists can be created on the router?

Ans: Only one **ACL** per interface, per protocol, per direction is allowed.

Q) What is the difference between Named ACL and Numbered ACL?

Ans: 1) Numbered ACL is created by using a number; Named ACL is created by using a name.

2) Removing of specific statement is not possible in Numbered ACL, but it is possible in Named ACL.

Q) What is the difference between the Access-group and Access-class commands?

Ans: The Access-group command is used to filter traffic on the interface

Access-class command is used to filter traffic on lines (vty, console, aux)

Q) Is ACL case sensitive or not?

Ans: Case Sensitive

NAT (NETWORK ADDRESS TRANSLATION)

Network Address Translation (NAT) is a method used to map one or more local IP addresses to one or more global IP addresses and vice versa. This process allows multiple devices on a local network to access the internet using a single public IP address. NAT operates on a router or firewall and translates the private IP addresses of devices within a local network to a public IP address before sending packets to an external network.

Advantages:

Conserves IP Addresses: NAT helps conserve the limited number of available public IP addresses by allowing multiple devices to share a single public IP

Provides Privacy: By hiding the internal IP addresses, NAT provides a layer of privacy for devices on a local network

Simplifies Network Management: NAT eliminates the need for address renumbering when a network evolves

Disadvantages:

Switching Path Delays: NAT can introduce delays in the switching path due to the translation process.

Application Compatibility: Some applications may not function correctly when NAT is enabled

Complicates Tunneling Protocols: NAT can complicate protocols like IPsec, which rely on end-to-end connectivity.

Types of NAT

There are three types of address translation.

Static NAT – translates one private IP address to a public one. The public IP address is always the same.

Dynamic NAT – private IP addresses are mapped to the pool of public IP addresses.

Port Address Translation (PAT) – one public IP address is used for all internal devices, but a different port is assigned to each private IP address. Also known as **NAT Overload**.

www.networkprofessional.net   training@networkprofessional.net   774-253-62281508-859-0440

STATIC NETWORK ADDRESS TRANSLATION PROJECT TASK 9

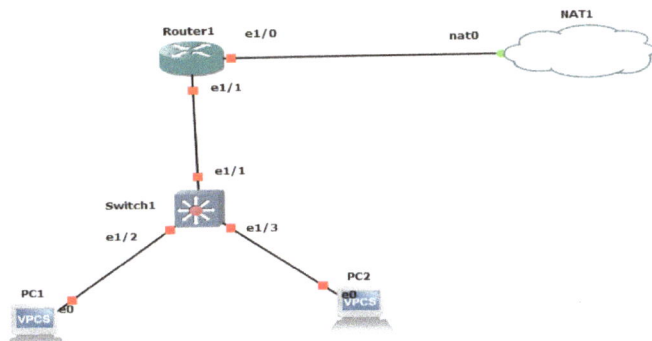

Static NAT Configuration

C1 Cloud Configuration

Right-click on cloud/configure and add your physical NIC. This configuration made internet access available to every device in this topology.

Step-by-Step NAT Configuration:

Since this is a test lab, I will use 192.168.1.0/24 network as a public IP and 10.1.1.0/24 as a local network.

Step-1:Define inside and outside interfaces

R1 (config) #**hostname Router_1**
Router_1 (confi#**int e1/0**
Router_1 (config-if)# **ip add**
Router_1 (config-if)#**no shut**
Router_1 (config-if)#**ex**
Router_1 (config)#**int e1/1**
Router_1 (config-if)#**ip add**
Router_1 (config-if)#**ip address 10.1.1.1 255.255.255.0**
Router_1 (config-if)#**ip nat inside**
Router_1 (config-if)#**ex**

Router_1 (config)#int e1 /0
Router_1 (config-if)#**ipnat outside**
Router_1 (config-if)#**exit**
Router_1 (config)#**ip route** 0.0.0.0 0.0.0.0 192.168.1.1 (For internet access)

Ensure that the router is configured to use the correct DNS server.

Router_1(config)#**ipdomain-lookup**
Router-1(config)**ip name-server 192.168.1.1**

Do a ping test to 8.8.8.8, Google.com, Facebook.com, and 4.2.2.

Step 2: Permit local IPs using Access-list

Create an access list that permits the hosts that will access the outside network/internet:

common error(config)#access-list 1 permit 10.1.1.0 0.0.0.255

Step 3: Configure Static NAT

Router_1(config)#**int e1 /0**

Router_1(config-if)#**ipnat outside**

Router_1(config-if)#**ipnat inside** source static **10.1.1.10 192.168.1.100**

NAT Verification Command:

From any host, ping any public IP, e.g., 4.2.2.2, and then use the command "Show ip nat translation" that will show the IP mapping.

Dynamic NAT Configuration

R1(config)#**access-list 1 permit 10.1.1.0 0.0.0.255**

R1(config)**ip nat pool global-ips 192.168.1.100 192.168.1.200 netmask 255.255.255.0**

R1(config)#**ip nat inside source list 1 pool global-ips**

Interview Questions on NAT

Q. Explain in detail the concept of NAT

Answer:

NAT (Network Address Translation) is a technique used to translate private IP addresses to public IP addresses, allowing devices on a private network to communicate with the internet

Q. Why is NAT used?

Answer: NAT is used for a few key reasons:

IP Address Conservation: With the limited number of IPv4 addresses, NAT helps conserve public IP addresses by allowing multiple devices to share one.

Security: NAT hides the internal network's structure and IP addresses, making it harder for external attackers to target specific devices.

Flexibility: NAT allows for easy network renumbering and migration.

Q. What are the different types of NAT?

Ans; Mainly 3 Static NAT, Dynamic NAT, and PAT-Port Address Translation (Overload)

VPN- VIRTUAL PRIVATE NETWORK

A **VPN (Virtual Private Network)** is a service that creates a secure, encrypted connection over the internet between your device and a remote server operated by the VPN provider. It's like a secure tunnel that hides your online activity, location, and data from prying eyes.

Key Purposes of a VPN:

1. **Privacy Protection**: Masks your IP address, making your online actions harder to trace.
2. **Data Encryption**: Encrypts data so it can't be read by hackers or your internet service provider (ISP).
3. **Remote Access**: Allows users (e.g., employees) to securely connect to a corporate network from remote locations.
4. **Bypass Censorship and Geo-blocks**: Access websites and services restricted in your location.

How It Works (Simplified):

1. You connect to the internet through VPN client software.
2. The VPN encrypts your data and sends it through a secure tunnel to the VPN server.
3. The VPN server then accesses the internet on your behalf, masking your real IP

Types of VPN

Remote Access VPN

Allows users to connect to a private network from a remote location, like connecting to a corporate network from home.

Client-to-Site VPN- Lets remote users access the corporate network with VPN clients. Once the Remote Access VPN is established, the remote user, by default, will not be able to access anything else on the Internet except the Corporate LAN network. This behavior can be altered by configuring the "split tunneling" feature on the Firewall (or Router), which, however, is not recommended for security purposes.

Clientless Mode. This lets users establish a secure remote access VPN tunnel using just a Web browser. There is no need for a software or hardware VPN client. However, only limited applications can be accessed remotely.

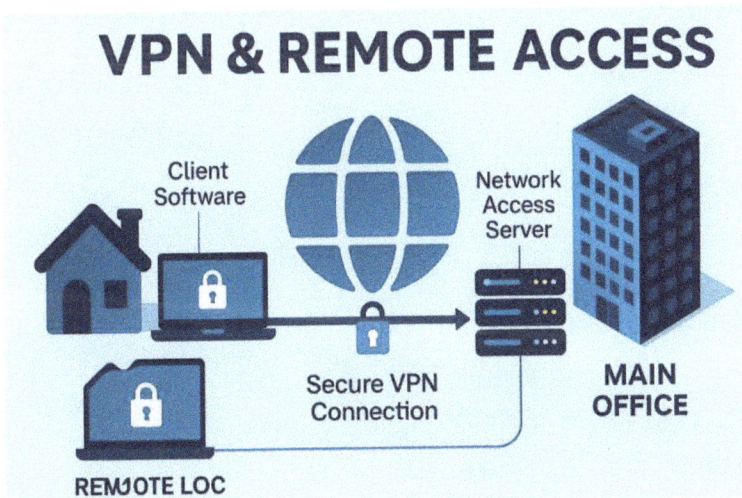

Site-to-Site VPN

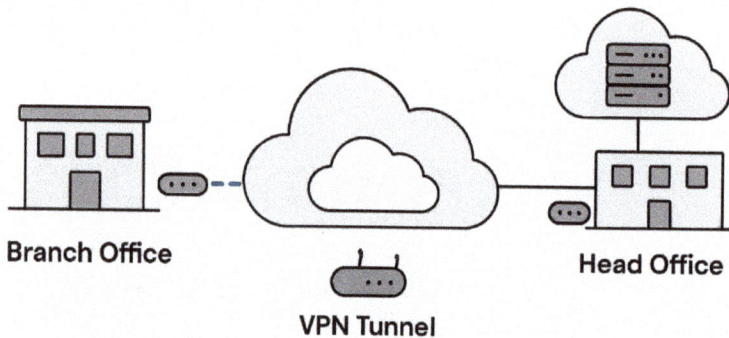

Site-to-site VPNs are ideal for companies with multiple offices needing secure communication, while remote access VPNs are better for individual users working from home or on business trips.

Purpose: Connect multiple networks together as if they were one.

Site-to-Site VPN

Branch Office

VPN Tunnel

Head Office

Provider Provisioned VPN (PPVPN) - MPLS VPN

- L2VPN, L3VPN, VPLS, PPTP, L2F, L2TP

Customer Provisioned VPNs- Secure VPNs

- IPSec- Site-to-Site VPN- Securely and transparently connects remote locations with your network.

GENERIC ROUTING ENCAPSULATION (GRE)

GRE VPN- Cisco originally developed Generic Routing Encapsulation (GRE), but later on, it was standardized and is now being used by many other vendors. If you have two separate LAN networks with private IP addresses, you can create a GRE VPN tunnel between them over the Internet and allow the two private LAN subnets to communicate. However, one of the main differences between GRE and traditional IPSEC is that GRE VPN does NOT provide encryption or any other security to the packets compared to IPSEC VPN. The best option for GRE VPN is to combine it with IPSEC. This means that we can protect the GRE Tunnel inside an IPSEC Tunnel, thus providing security as well (see diagram below)

Site-to-Site GRE/IPSEC VPN

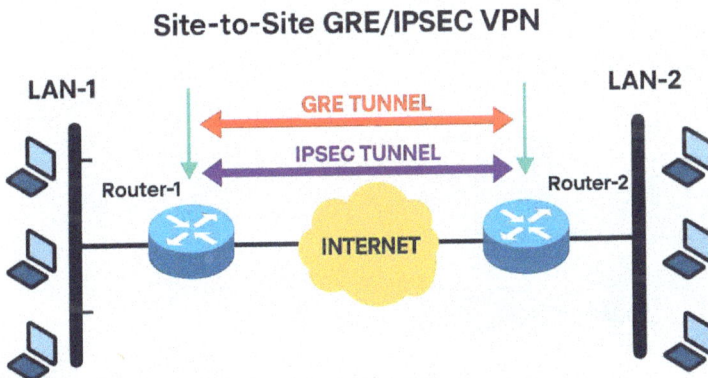

DM VPN- DMVPN stands for Dynamic Multipoint VPN. Is a Cisco-developed solution that simplifies the creation of scalable and dynamic VPNs between multiple sites over the internet. It uses a **hub-and-spoke** model, where the **hub router** acts as the central point and dynamically helps establish **on-demand, direct tunnels (spoke-to-spoke)** when needed.

DMVPN

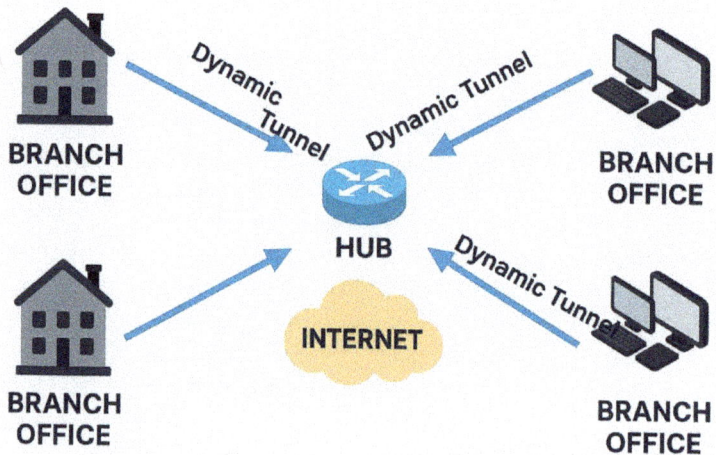

VPN CATEGORIES

1 Policy-Based VPN
(Native IPSEC)

Supported on Cisco + Routers

2 Route-Based VPN

Supported on Cisco Routers only

4 SSL-Based VPN WP)
(WebVPN)

Supported on Cisco Routers only

4 Dynamic Multipoint
VPN (DMVPN)

PRACTICAL APPLICATIONS

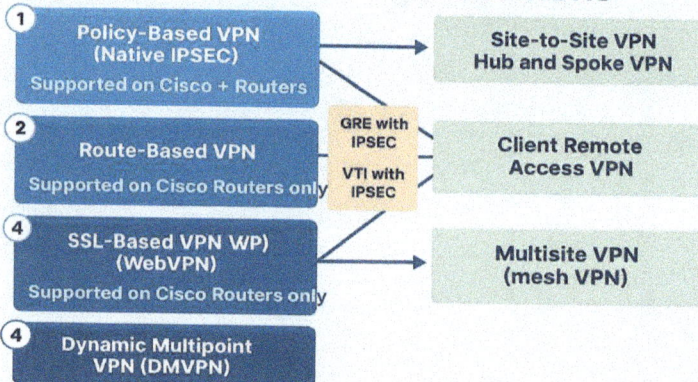

Site-to-Site VPN
Hub and Spoke VPN

GRE with IPSEC

VTI with IPSEC

Client Remote
Access VPN

Multisite VPN
(mesh VPN)

IPSEC SITE TO SITE VPN WITH CISCO ROUTERS

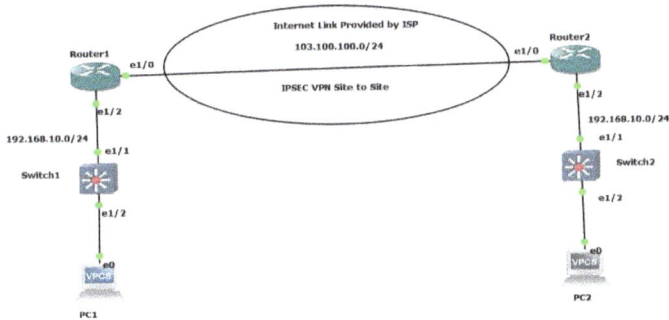

Global Configuration

1. Configure a hostname for all the devices
2. Disable the DNS lookup feature.
3. Assign R@ng as the Secret password.

Console Port

4. Configure the console port on all devices to log input synchronously
5. Set password to N
6. Configure the idling timeout to 10 minutes and 40 minutes

VTY Ports

7. Allow 16 concurrent sessions of remote access
8. Configure the vty ports to log input synchronously
9. Set password to C
10. Configure idling timeout to 30 minutes and 90 seconds
11. Save config

VLAN Configuration

12. Use the default VLAN for the Access Network
13. Create a network for each of the offices on the topology.
14. Assign static IP addresses for the PCs based on their respective network.

Network Routing

15. Use a Static routing protocol to route your network from one destination to another

PCs IP Assignment

16. Assign an IP address to the

PC1 192.168.10.3/24

PC2 192.168.20.3/24

This a security form you fill anytime you are setting up a new vpn tunnel to specify the parameters you are going to use for the tunnel

Step1: Set up ISAKMP Policy(IKE) – ISAKMP PHASE 1 POLICY)

Apply this on both HeadOffice and Branch Office

Use below Parameters

3DES- The encryption method to be used for Phase 1

Sha- The has algorithm

Pre-share- Use Pre-share key as authentication method

Group 2 – Diffie-Helman group to be used

86400- Session key lifetime

Headoffice(config)#**crypto isakmp policy 1**
Headoffice(config-isakmp)#**authentication pre-share**
Headoffice(config-isakmp)#**encryption 3des**
Headoffice(config-isakmp)#**hash sha**
Headoffice(config-isakmp)#**group 2**
Headoffice(config-isakmp)# **lifetime 86400**

BranchOffice(config)#**crypto isakmp policy 1**
BranchOffice(config-isakmp)#**authentication pre-share**
BranchOffice(config-isakmp)#**encryption 3des**
BranchOffice(config-isakmp)#**hash sha**
BranchOffice(config-isakmp)#**group 2**
BranchOffice(config-isakmp)#**lifetime 86400**

Step-2 Create VPN Tunnel Group

Pre-share key is to be configured here for the site-to-site connection

Pre-Share= HQ-to-BR

Headoffice(config)#crypto isakmp key 0 HQ-to-BR address 103.100.100.2

BranchOffice(config)#crypto isakmp key 0 HQ-to-BR address 103.100.100.1

Step 3: Create IPsec Transform set (ISKAMP PHASE 2 POLICY) PHASE 2 is also called IPsec Policy

Use a transform name at Head office = HQ-TS

Use a transform name at Branch office = BR-TS

Headoffice(config)# crypto ipsec transform-set HQ-TS esp-3des esp-md5-hmac

BranchOffice(config)# crypto ipsec transform-set BR-TS esp-3des esp-md5-hmac

The above command defines the following

ESP-3DES- Encryption Method

MD5- Hashing algorithm

Step4: Create ACL for the VPN tunnel

Define the traffic we would like the router to pass through the VPN tunnel

Headoffice(config)#ip access-list extended ACL-VPN

Headoffice(config-ext-nacl)#permit ip 192.168.10.0 0.0.0.255 192.168.20.0 192.168.20.0 0.0.0.255

BranchOffice(config)#ip access-list extended ACL-VPN

BranchOffice(config)# permit ip 192.168.20.0 0.0.0.255 192.168.20.0 192.168.10.0 0.0.0.255

Step5: Configure and apply Crypto Map to the public interface
On Head Office

Headoffice(config)#crypto map HQ-VPN 1 ipsec-isakmp

Headoffice(config)#crypto-map)#set transform-set HQ-TS

Headoffice(config)#crypto-map)#match address ACL-VPN

Headoffice(config)#set peer 103.100.100.2

Headoffice(config-crypto-map)#int e1 /0

Headoffice(config-if)#crypto map HQ-VPN

Headoffice(config-if)#

*May   23   23:46:46.584:   %CRYPTO-6-ISAKMP_ON_OFF: ISAKMP is ON

BranchOffice

BranchOffice(config)#crypto map BR-VPN 1 ipsec-isakmp

% NOTE: This new crypto map will remain disabled until a peer

BranchOffice(config-crypto-map)#set transform-set BR-TS

BranchOffice(config-crypto-map)#match address ACL-VPN

BranchOffice(config-crypto-map)# set peer 103.100.100.1

BranchOffice(config-crypto-map)#int e1 /0

BranchOffice(config-if)#crypto map BR-VPN

Verification

To bring up the tunnel, we need to ping the IP address of the host in the head office to the remote office

PC1 > ping 192.168.20.3

192.168.20.3 icmp_seq=1 timeout

84 bytes from 192.168.20.3 icmp_seq=2 ttl=62 time=3.013 ms

84 bytes from 192.168.20.3 icmp_seq=3 ttl=62 time=1.233 ms

84 bytes from 192.168.20.3 icmp_seq=4 ttl=62 time=1.415 ms

Headoffice#show crypto isakmp sa

IPv4 Crypto ISAKMP SA

Dst	Src	State	conn-id	Status
203.200.200.2	203.200.200.1	QM_IDLE	1001	ACTIVE

If the state is MM-NO_STATE – not working

Headoffice# show crypto ipsec sa

remote   ident   (addr/mask/prot/port):
(192.168.20.0/255.255.255.0/0/0)

current_peer 203.200.200.2 port 500

PERMIT, flags={origin_is_acl,}

#pkts encaps: 4, #pkts encrypt: 4, #pkts digest: 4

#pkts decaps: 4, #pkts decrypt: 4, #pkts verify: 4

GRE VPN – Site-to-Site

This is the simplest scenario of having two sites connected over the Internet with a GRE tunnel protected by IPSEC. The IPSEC protection provides security, and it's highly recommended, but it's not a requirement for having network connectivity between the two sites. You can have only a GRE tunnel if you want without IPSEC. The major advantage of using GRE is that it can transport multicast traffic and dynamic routing protocols between the two sites.

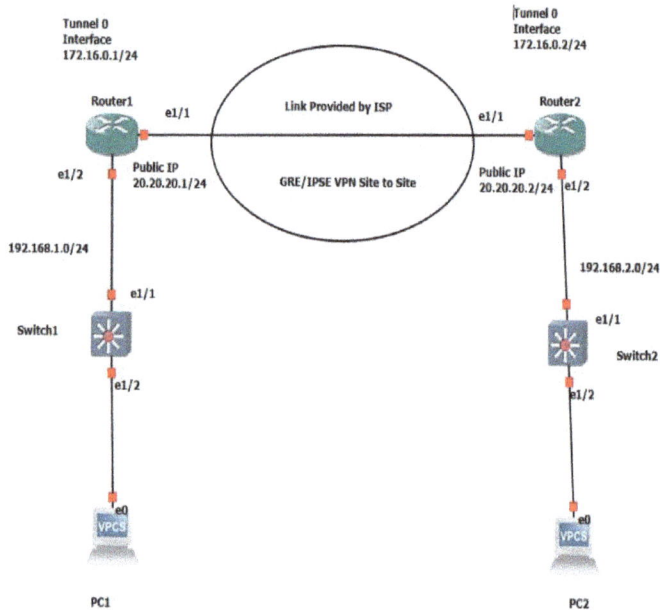

Create your LAN and WAN to ping the local and direct connected interface with no routing protocol.

Step1: Creating a Cisco GRE tunnel

GRE tunnel uses a tunnel interface on the router with an IP address where packets are encapsulated and decapsulated as they enter or exit the GRE tunnel

interface Tunnel0

IP address 172.16.10.1 255.255.255.0

ip mtu 1400

ip tcp adjust-mss 1360

tunnel source 20.20.20.1

tunnel destination 20.20.20.2

Next, we must create the Tunnel 0 interface on R2:

interface Tunnel0

IP address 172.16.10.1 255.255.255.0

ip mtu 1400

ip tcp adjust-mss 1360

tunnel source 20.20.20.1

tunnel destination 20.20.20.2

R2(config-if)# **tunnel destination 20.20.20.1**

R2's Tunnel interface is configured with the appropriate tunnel source and destination IP address. As with R1, R2 router will inform us that the Tunnel0 interface **is up:**

Step: 2 CREATING A ROUTING NETWORKS THROUGH THE GRE TUNNEL

R1(config)# ip route 192.168.2.0 255.255.255.0 172.16.10.2

R2(config)# ip route 192.168.1.0 255.255.255.0 172.16.10.1

PC1 > ping 192.168.2.3

84 bytes from 192.168.2.3 icmp_seq=1 ttl=62 time=3.357 ms

84 bytes from 192.168.2.3 icmp_seq=2 ttl=62 time=1.625 ms

Step 3: Securing the GRE tunnel with IPsec

We use IPsec to add an encryption layer to secure the GRE tunnel

Set up ISAKMP Policy(IKE) – ISAKMP PHASE 1

Headoffice(config)#**crypto isakmp policy 1**

Headoffice(config-isakmp)#**authentication pre-share**

Headoffice(config-isakmp)#**encryption 3des**

Headoffice(config-isakmp)#**hash md5**

Headoffice(config-isakmp)#**group 2**

Headoffice(config-isakmp)# **lifetime 86400**

NB: Repeat Same on the Branch Office

Step 4: Create IPsec Transform (ISAKMP Phase 2)

Headoffice(config)#**crypto ipsec transform-set TS esp-3des esp-md5-hmac**

Headoffice(config)# **mode transport**

BranchOffice(config)#**crypto ipsec transform-set TS esp-3des esp-md5-hmac**

BranchOffice(config)# **mode transport**

Step5: Create IPsec Profile to connect the previously defined ISAKMP and IPsec configuration together

Headoffice(config)# **crypto ipsec profile protect-gre**

Headoffice(config)# **set security-association lifetime seconds 86400**

Headoffice(config)# **Set transform-set TS**

Headoffice(config)# **int t0**

Headoffice(config)# **tunnel protection ipsec profile protect-gre**

NB Apply same on the Branch Office

Do a ping test to verify if the tunnel is up

Headoffice#show crypto isakmp sa

IPv4 Crypto ISAKMP SA

Dst	Src	State	conn-id	Status
20.20.20.2	20.20.20.1	QM_IDLE	1001	ACTIVE

As you can see above, the output fields "pkts encrypt" and "pkts decrypt" show indeed that we have packets being encrypted and decrypted bi-directionally

Important Points to Remember:

- As you have seen above, in Route-Based VPNs there is no need to define Interesting Traffic using ACLs as we did in Policy-Based VPNs.
- Instead of defining which Interesting Traffic will be encrypted, configure static (or dynamic) routing to tell the router that the remote LAN network will be reachable via the other-end of the GRE Tunnel Interface. All traffic routed through the Tunnel Interface will be placed in the VPN and also protected by IPSEC. That's why we call this VPN type as "Route-Based" VPN.
- There is no need to exclude Interesting Traffic from NAT operation

INTRODUCTION OF FIREWALL IN COMPUTER NETWORK

A Network Firewall may be a Hardware or a Software device - It protects a computer network from unauthorized access. Network firewalls guard an internal LAN network from malicious access from the outside/unsecured zone, such as malware-infested websites or vulnerable ports. The main purpose of a firewall is to separate a secured area (Higher security Zone / Inside Network) from a less secure area (Low-security Zone / Outside Network, etc.) and to control communication between the two. Firewall also controls inbound and outbound communications across devices.

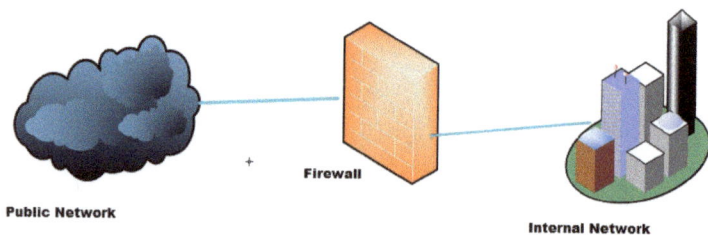

Public Network   Firewall   Internal Network

Firewall Products

Cisco ASA

Fortinet FortiGate

Cisco Firepower NGFW

Palo-Alto Networks Next-Generation Firewall

Juniper SRX Series

pfSense

SonicWALL Firewalls

Untangle NG Firewall

Competitors to Cisco ASA

Cisco ASA with Firepower services is a premium security product for Enterprise Networks, and according to gartner.com and spiceworks.com there are only three direct competitors to these Cisco products. They are Palo Alto, Fortinet, and Checkpoint.

Palo Alto

Palo Alto's next-generation firewalls provide similar features to Cisco ASA firewalls through their PAN-OS operating system. The Palo Alto firewalls and firewall clusters can be managed by their Firewall management system, known as Panorama.

Fortinet

Fortinet has a very large range of firewall models aimed at every size network, from entry-level to cloud data centers. These firewalls run the FortiGate operating system. Fortinet is one of the fastest-growing security firms worldwide, and they manufacture all kinds of security products, such as firewalls, antivirus, email security, SIEM, Wi-Fi, etc.

Checkpoint

Checkpoint has taken a unified approach to network security through a suite of products that include Next Generation Firewalls known as the Infinity architecture.

This architecture is made up of five sections, which are Quantum, Cloud Guard, Harmony, and Infinity Vision, which surrounds their Security Intelligence center known as Infinity Threat Cloud. Checkpoint has a large offering of 15 different Firewall models.

Advantages of Using Firewall

1. **Protection from unauthorized access:** Firewalls can be set up to restrict incoming traffic from particular IP addresses or networks, preventing hackers or other malicious actors from easily accessing a network or system. Protection from unwanted access.
2. **Prevention of malware and other threats:** Malware and other threat prevention: Firewalls can be set up to block traffic linked to known malware or other security concerns, assisting in the defense against these kinds of attacks.
3. **Control of network access:** By limiting access to specified individuals or groups for particular servers or applications, firewalls can be used to restrict access to particular network resources or services.
4. **Monitoring of network activity:** Firewalls can be set up to record and keep track of all network activity. This information is essential for identifying and looking into security problems and other kinds of shady behavior.
5. **Regulation compliance:** Many industries are bound by rules that demand the usage of firewalls or other security measures. Organizations can comply with these rules and prevent any fines or penalties by using a firewall.
6. **Network segmentation:** By using firewalls to split up a bigger network into smaller subnets, the attack surface is reduced, and the security level is raised.

Types of Firewall Base How to Deploy

1. **Dedicated hardware appliances** are generally used in data centers.
2. **Software on a machine** as used by home users. e.g., Windows Firewall
3. **Managed firewall services** have many options, including a premises-based, network-based, or **cloud-based service (Firewall as a Service).** In this case, the firewall manufacturer or service provider takes care of the network and is responsible for firewall administration, log monitoring, etc.

Types of Firewalls Based on Method of Operation

1. **Packet Filtering/Stateless:** As the name suggests, the user can either allow or drop packets based on source and destination IP, IP protocol ID, etc., from entering the internal network. This type of filtering works at the network transport layer.

2. **Proxy:** It offers more security than other types of filtering. In proxy filtering, the client connects with a proxy instead of a target system and initiates a new connection. This makes it harder for an attacker to discover the network, as they are not getting a response from the target system.

3. **Stateful Inspection:** In this type of inspection, systems maintain a state table (maintains active connections), analyze incoming and outgoing packets, and drop accordingly.

4. **Application Layer Firewalls:** These firewalls can examine application layer (of OSI model) information like an HTTP request. If you find some suspicious application that can be responsible for harming our network or that is not safe for our network, then it gets blocked right away.

5. **Next-generation Firewalls:** These firewalls are called intelligent firewalls. These firewalls can perform all the tasks that are performed by the other types of firewalls that we learned previously, but on top of that, they include additional features like application awareness and control, integrated intrusion prevention, and cloud-delivered threat intelligence.

FIREWALL MODES

Cisco ASA can be used in 2 modes, which are Routed Mode and Transparent Mode.

Routed Firewall Mode

In routed mode, the ASA is considered to be a router in the network. It can use OSPF or RIP (in single context mode). Routed mode supports many interfaces. Each interface is on a different subnet. The ASA acts as a router between connected networks, and each interface requires an IP address on a different subnet. This is the default working mode of Cisco ASA.

Transparent Firewall Mode

ASA in Transparent firewall mode works as a Layer 2 switch/bridge while still providing firewall benefits (intrusion prevention, packet inspection, etc). In this mode ASA acts like a "bump in the wire," or a "stealth firewall," and is not seen as a router to connected devices. Only the management interface can receive an IP address when ASA is working in Transparent Mode. The ASA connects the same network between its interfaces. Because the firewall is not a routed hop, you can easily introduce a transparent firewall into an existing network without having to make any changes to the network.

CISCO ASA FIREWALL SECURITY LEVELS

The Cisco ASA Firewall uses so-called "security levels" that indicate how trusted an interface is compared to another interface. The higher the security level, the more trusted the interface is. Each interface on the ASA is a security zone, so by using these security levels, we have different trust levels for our security zones.

An interface with a high-security level can access an interface with a low-security level, but the other way around is not possible unless we configure an access list that permits this traffic.

Here are a couple of examples of security levels:

- **Security level 0**: This is the lowest security level there is on the ASA, and by default, it is assigned to the "outside" interface. Since there is no lower security level, this means that traffic from the outside is unable to reach any of our interfaces unless we permit it within an access list.

- **Security level 100**: This is the highest security level on our ASA, and by default, this is assigned to the "inside" interface. We usually use this for our "LAN." Since this is the highest security level, by default, it can reach all the other interfaces.

- **Security level 1 – 99**: We can create any other security levels that we want. For example, we can use security level 50 for our DMZ. This means that traffic is allowed from our inside network to the DMZ (security level 100 -> 50) and also from the DMZ to the outside (security level 50 -> 0). Traffic from the DMZ, however, can't go to the inside (without an access list) because traffic from security level 50 is not allowed to reach security level 100. You can create as many security levels as you want…

Rules

In short, this is how the security levels work:

- Traffic from a **higher security level to a lower security level is allowed**. For example, traffic from the inside is allowed to reach the outside. Of course, it's possible to restrict this with access lists.

- Traffic from a **lower security level to a higher security level is not allowed**. This could be traffic from the outside headed towards the inside. You can also change this with an access list. This might be useful if you have servers in the DMZ that you want to reach from the outside.

- Traffic between interfaces with the **same security level is not allowed**. For example, if you have an interface called "DMZ1" with security level 50 and another one called "DMZ2" with the same security level, then traffic between the two will be dropped. You can change this behavior with the global **same-security-traffic permit inter-interface** command.

- Our LAN is our trusted network, which has a high security level. The WAN is untrusted, so it will have a low-security level. This means that traffic from our LAN > WAN will be permitted. Traffic from the WAN to our LAN will be denied. Since the firewall is stateful, it keeps track of outgoing connections and will permit the return traffic from our LAN.
- If you want to make an exception and permit traffic from the WAN to the LAN, then this can be accomplished with an access list.
- Most companies will have one or more servers that should be reachable from the Internet. Perhaps a mail or web server. Instead of placing these on the INSIDE, we use a third zone called the **DMZ (Demilitarized Zone)**. Take a look at the picture below:

ISP Connectivity & Redundancy Options

These are different design topologies where we describe how a customer is connected to one or more ISPs.

Various ISP Connection Types

- **Single homed**: you are connected to a single ISP using a single link.
- **Dual homed**: you are connected to a single ISP using dual links.
- **Single multi-homed**: you are connected to two ISPs using single links.
- **Dual multi-homed**: you are connected to two ISPs using dual links

Single Homed

The single-homed design means you have a single connection to a single ISP. With this design, you don't need BGP since there is only one exit path in your network. You might as well just use a static default route that points to the ISP.

The advantage of a single-homed link is that it's cost-effective. The disadvantage is that you don't have any redundancy. Your link is a single point of failure, but so is using a single ISP.

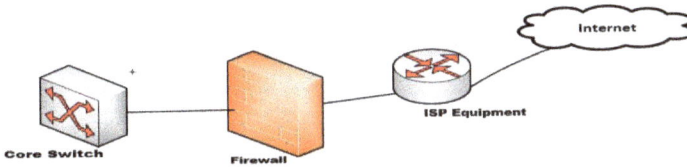

Single Multi-homed

Multihomed means we are connected to at least two different ISPs. The simplest design looks like this:

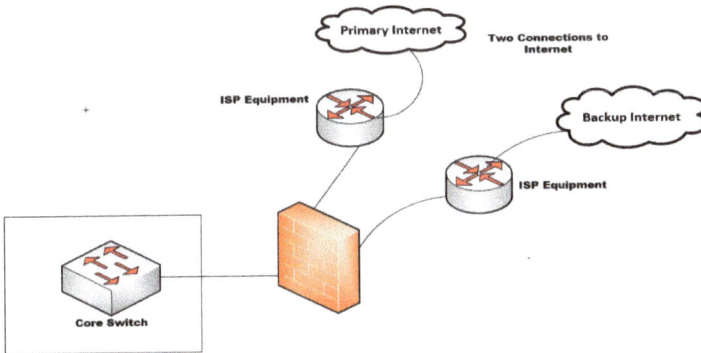

Firewall redundancy

Using just a single ASA is a single point of failure and usually catastrophically reflects in the network when the device experiences common setbacks such as hardware issues, link/cable problems, or just a simple misconfiguration.

Therefore, using a second ASA to the primary one will provide a backup solution in case something goes wrong with the active unit.

Overall, the deployment of multiple firewalls offers a variety of benefits, ranging from greater performance to enhanced security. If your security environment warrants this type of scenario, it's definitely an option worth considering.

Common Deployment scenarios

1) Fault tolerance and load balancing
2) Enhanced perimeter protection
3) Protected subnets Redundancy firewall Design

Deployment scenarios and benefits

1. Fault tolerance and load balancing Redundancy Firewall Design

Many organizations choose to implement dual firewalls in a parallel fashion, as shown in the figure below. When the router is properly configured, this provides the added benefits of fault tolerance and load balancing. Both firewalls should be configured to be "fail-safe;" that is, in the event of a failure, they should automatically block all traffic. When configured in this fashion, the firewalls provide fault tolerance; when one fails, the other is able to carry the network traffic and keep the failure transparent to users.

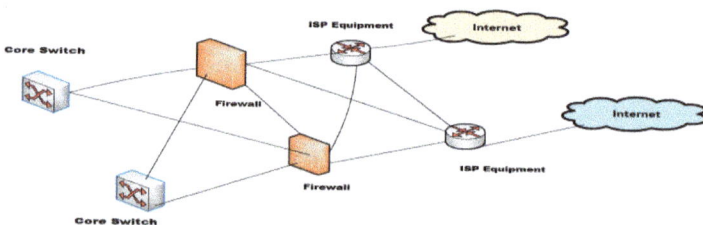

Enhanced perimeter protection Redundancy Firewall design

It's also possible to deploy the two firewalls in a series circuit, as shown in the illustration below. When configured in this fashion, all traffic passing into or out of the network must pass through both firewalls.

This setup is sometimes deployed in high-security environments to protect against firewall-specific vulnerabilities. In this case, the two firewalls are from different vendors and may even run on different operating systems.

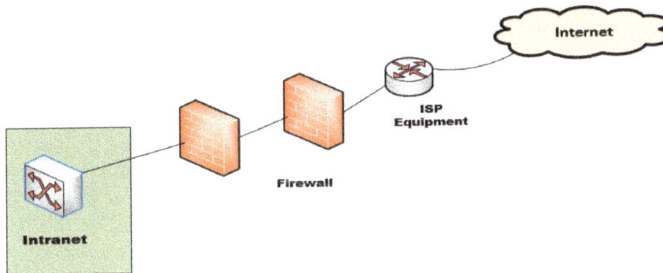

Protected subnets Redundancy firewall Design

The final scenario we'll discuss is shown in the figure below. In this case, secondary firewall(s) are used to protect subnets of the internal network that have greater security requirements than the network as a whole.

This type of scenario may be used, for example, to provide an accounting department with added protection for sensitive financial data they wish to protect from other internal users.

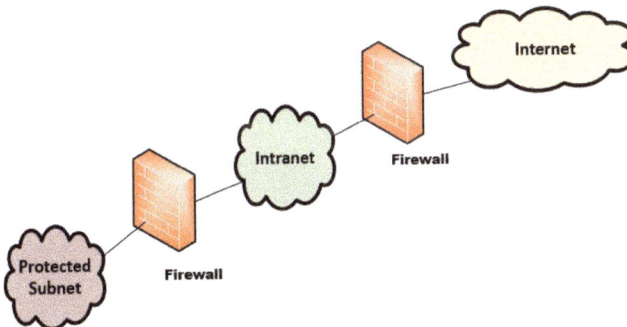

Phase 1 Configuration and its Purpose

Phase 1 of IPSec is used to establish a secure channel between the two peers that will be used for further data transmission. The ASAs will exchange secret keys, authenticate each other, and will negotiate about the IKE security policies. This is what happens in phase 1:

- Authenticate and protect the identities of the IPsec peers.
- Negotiate a matching IKE policy between IPsec peers to protect the IKE exchange.
- Perform an authenticated Diffie-Hellman exchange to have matching shared secret keys.
- Set up a secure tunnel for IKE phase 2.

Phase 2 Configuration and its Purpose

Once the secure tunnel from Phase 1 has been established, we will start Phase 2. In this phase, the two firewalls will negotiate about the IPsec security parameters that will be used to protect the traffic within the tunnel. In short, this is what happens in phase 2:

- Negotiate IPsec security parameters through the secure tunnel from phase 1.
- Establish IPsec security associations.
- Periodically renegotiates IPsec security associations for security.

SITE TO SITE IPSEC VPN PROJECT WITH CISCO ASA

Site-to-Site IPSEC VPN Project Task

Create IPsec site-to-site VPN using the Topology above

Step1. Open your ASDM for Site-1 > click Wizards > VPN wizard>site to site vpn> Next

Step2. Enter your Peer's IP address

Step-3 Select which traffic to encrypt

Step-4 Specify the PSK as Cisco

Step-4 Exempt NAT rule for the local address

Step-5 Go through the summary and edit when needed

Step-6 Repeat the same process using the same PSK and your Peer IP address

Step-7. Let's test the tunnel by pinging from a user

USER1#**ping 10.10.12.2**

Type escape sequence to abort.

Sending 5, 100-byte ICMP Echos to 10.10.12.2, timeout is 2 seconds:

.!!!!

Success rate is 80 percent (4/5), round-trip min/avg/max = 21/31/38 ms

```
Site-1-ASA# show crypto isakmp sa

There are no IKEv1 SAs

IKEv2 SAs:

Session-id:1, Status:UP-ACTIVE, IKE count:1, CHILD count:1

Tunnel-id          Local              Remote      Status      Role
  2889995    102.100.100.1/500   102.100.100.2/500   READY   INITIATOR
      Encr: AES-CBC, keysize: 256, Hash: SHA96, DH Grp:5, Auth sign: PSK, Auth verify: PS
K
      Life/Active Time: 86400/552 sec
Child sa: local selector  10.10.11.0/0 - 10.10.11.255/65535
          remote selector 10.10.12.0/0 - 10.10.12.255/65535
          ESP spi in/out: 0x44b661fd/0x206f7ba9
```

```
Site-1-ASA# show crypto ipsec sa
interface: outside
    Crypto map tag: outside_map, seq num: 1, local addr: 102.100.100.1

    access-list outside_cryptomap_2 extended permit ip 10.10.11.0 255.255.255.0 10.10.1
2.0 255.255.255.0
        local ident (addr/mask/prot/port): (10.10.11.0/255.255.255.0/0/0)
        remote ident (addr/mask/prot/port): (10.10.12.0/255.255.255.0/0/0)
        current_peer: 102.100.100.2


        #pkts encaps: 4, #pkts encrypt: 4, #pkts digest: 4
        #pkts decaps: 4, #pkts decrypt: 4, #pkts verify: 4
        #pkts compressed: 0, #pkts decompressed: 0
        #pkts not compressed: 4, #pkts comp failed: 0, #pkts decomp failed: 0
        #pre-frag successes: 0, #pre-frag failures: 0, #fragments created: 0
        #PMTUs sent: 0, #PMTUs rcvd: 0, #decapsulated frgs needing reassembly: 0
        #TFC rcvd: 0, #TFC sent: 0
        #Valid ICMP Errors rcvd: 0, #Invalid ICMP Errors rcvd: 0
        #send errors: 0, #recv errors: 0

        local crypto endpt.: 102.100.100.1/500, remote crypto endpt.: 102.100.100.2/500
        path mtu 1500, ipsec overhead 74(44), media mtu 1500
        PMTU time remaining (sec): 0, DF policy: copy-df
        ICMP error validation: disabled, TFC packets: disabled
        current outbound spi: 206F7BA9
```

CISCO VERSUS JUNIPER COMPARISON

There are three main aspects t in comparing Cisco and Juniper routers.

1. Impact of Market Share

One thing highlighted by a Cisco and Juniper router comparison is the fact that Cisco has a larger share of the overall router market. Because of that, there are more certified Cisco service engineers and more online support resources compared with Juniper for troubleshooting hardware issues.

2. Two Different Modular Configuration Architectures

Comparing Cisco vs Juniper routers also shows that although modular Cisco and Juniper routers both have mechanisms for customizing port configurations and modules, the systems are very different. Cisco uses line cards, which are inserted directly into the router chassis, compared with Juniper routers, which use a multi-layered system involving Modular Port Concentrators (MPC) and Modular Interface Cards (MIC). In a Juniper router chassis, the MPC goes into the chassis, and then multiple MICs are inserted into the MPC.

3. Optical Transceiver Form Factors

Another key distinction pointed out by a Cisco vs. Juniper router comparison is that Cisco has its own proprietary **CPAK** optical transceiver form factor, which supports up to 100G Ethernet. Although Juniper's routers support a combination of optical transceivers that support 100G Ethernet, including **CFP, CFP2, and QSFP28**, they are not compatible with **CPAK** optics.

JUNIPER SWITCH MODELS

JUNIPER HAS 2 PRODUCT FAMILY EX SERIES, AND QFX SERIES SWITCHES

EX Switches Product

EX Series switches are high-performance access and distribution/core-layer devices for enterprise branch, campus, and data center networks.

Models: EX4400, EX4300, EX3400, EX2300, EX9200, EX4600

QFX Switches Product

QFX Series Switches deliver industry-leading throughput and scalability, an extensive routing stack, and the open programmability of the Junos OS. With QFX, you'll find premier solutions for data center spine-and-leaf, campus distribution and core, and data center gateway and interconnect switching.

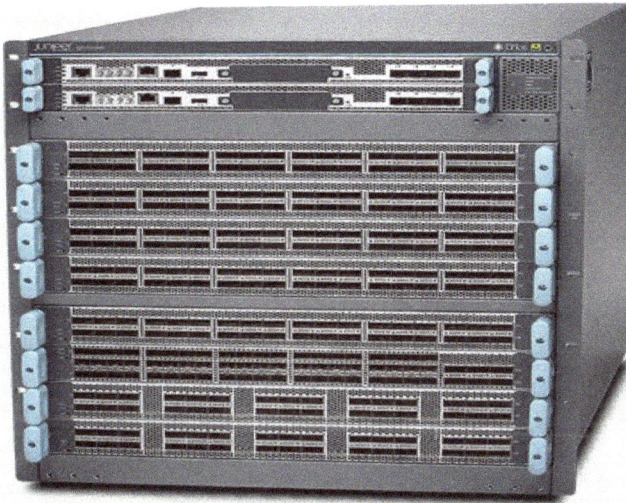

QFX Models: QFX5700, QFX5130, QTX1000, QFX10008 and 10016

JUNIPER ROUTER MODELS

The bulk of Juniper's routers fall under its MX Series, which covers enterprise, data center, and service provider networking environments. Juniper routers provide customers with a wide range of application scenarios, including branches, medium-sized businesses, large-size businesses, etc. Hot series are the Juniper **MX204/MX240/MX480** Routers**, MX2020 5G** routing platforms, **MX960 5G** platforms, and others.

MX204-R

MX480

JUNIPER LAB GUIDE _1 (MIXED ENVIRONMENT WITH STATIC ROUTING)

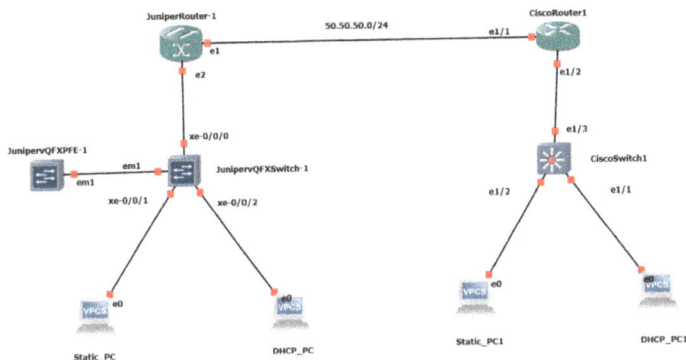

Before going into command details, you should know that there are different command modes on Juniper, like Cisco. So you must know about every command and where to type it. You can simply differentiate these modes into:

- Command-line interface (CLI)
- Configuration mode
- The CLI has two modes:
- **Operational mode**—Use this mode to display the current status of the device. In operational mode, you enter commands to monitor and troubleshoot the network.
- **Configuration mode**—Use this mode to configure the device. In this mode, you enter statements to configure all properties of the device.

How to log into the Juniper router:

Simply type user name and password; the default username and password for JunOS is **root** with no password.

Login: root

Password: (hit Enter)

1. Configure all network devices with the following basic information.

root@% cli	Command-line interface
root>	User | operational mode
root > set cli idle-timeout 60	Maximum idle time
root> configure /edit	Enter Configuration mode.
root#	Configuration mode.
root# set system host-name Internet_Router	Changes hostname
root # set system root-authentication plain-text-password	

Assigns **NPTC123** as secret

New password: nptc123

password

Retype new password: nptc123

root# set system services telnet	Telnet line
root# set system services ssh	SSH line
root# commit and-quit	save configuration

root@Internet__Router# edit system login	Change to edit system login
root@Juniper_Router# edit user user1	Add a new user account
root@Internet_Router# set full-name "user One"	Configure a full name for the account
root@Internet_Router# set class super-user	Configure class account
root@Internet_Router# set authentication plain-text-passwor	set a Password for the Acct
New password: nptc123	Retype new password: nptc123
root@Internet_Router# commit and-quit	To Save

Verification command

Show configuration | Cisco Show run

Show configuration | display set – Gives configuration to copy and paste

root@Internet_Router> show configuration

Last commit: 2022-03-04 22:48:16 UTC by root

version 12.1R1.9;

system {

   host-name Internet_Router;

   root-authentication {

     encrypted-password "1RJxlfE4b$BuYN/bLIMsZykyNmgpKzU.";   ##   SECRET-DATA

     }

```
    }
    user user1 {
        full-name user;
        uid 2001;
        class super-user;
        authentication {
            encrypted-password
"$1$PxA/R4vs$ex5QsSDZHeWYbFUgaknF4/";   ##   SECRET-
DATA
        }
    }
}
services {
    ssh;
    telnet;
}
syslog {
    user * {
```

root@Internet_Router> show configuration | display set

set version 12.1R1.9

set system host-name Internet_Router

set   system   root-authentication   encrypted-password
"1RJxIfE4b$BuYN/bLIMsZykyNmgpKzU."

set system login user user1 full-name user

set system login user user1 uid 2001

set system login user user1 class super-user

set system login user user1 authentication encrypted-password
"1PxA/R4vs$ex5QsSDZHeWYbFUgaknF4/"

set system services ssh

set system services telnet

set system syslog user * any emergency

set system syslog file messages any notice

set system syslog file messages authorization info

1. **Assign the IP address to the Router and describe the port and the network.**
root@Internet_Router# edit interfaces em2

[edit interfaces em2]

root@Internet_Router# set description Juniper Switch

root@Internet_Router# set vlan-tagging

[edit interfaces em2

root@Internet_Router# set unit 20 vlan-id 20

[edit interfaces em2

root@Internet_Router# set unit 20 family inet addresses 192.168.1.1/24

[edit interfaces em2]

root@Internet_Router# commit check

configuration check succeeds

root@Internet_Router# run show configuration | display set | match em2

set interfaces em2 description Juniper_Switch

set interfaces em2 vlan-tagging

set interfaces em2 unit 20 vlan-id 20

set interfaces em2 unit 20 family inet address 192.168.1.1/24

root@Internet_Router# run show interfaces terse em2

Interface	Admin	Link	Proto	Local	Remote
em2	up	up			
em2.20	up	up	inet	192.168.1.1/24	

1)   Configure both routers to act as DHCP server

root@Internet_Router> **edit**

root@Internet_Router#edit system services dhcp

set pool 192.168.1.0/24 address-range low 192.168.1.10 high 192.168.1.254 (Specify the pool)

set pool 192.168.1.0/24 default-lease-time 4320 (Configure default lease-time)

set pool 192.168.1.0/24 router 192.168.1.1 (Configure the default-router address)

Verification command

root@Internet_Router#commit and-quit

commit complete

Exiting configuration mode

root@Internet_Router> show configuration | display set | match DHCP

set system services dhcp pool 192.168.1.0/24 address-range low 192.168.1.10

set system services dhcp pool 192.168.1.0/24 address-range high 192.168.1.254

set system services dhcp pool 192.168.1.0/24 default-lease-time 4320

set system services dhcp pool 192.168.1.0/24 router 192.168.1.1

root@Internet_Router> delete system services dhcp (**To remove configuration and Rollback all works)**

root@Internet_Router# run show configuration | display set | match dhcp (Still show because the command was not commited)

set system services dhcp pool 192.168.1.0/24 address-range low 192.168.1.10

set system services dhcp pool 192.168.1.0/24 address-range high 192.168.1.254

set system services dhcp pool 192.168.1.0/24 default-lease-time 4320

set system services dhcp pool 192.168.1.0/24 router 192.168.1.1

[edit]

root@Internet_Router# commit

commit complete

[edit]

root@Internet_Router# run show configuration | display set | match dhcp

Now configuration is gone

[edit]

show system service dhcp binding (This show command gives you lease IPS)

How to log into the Juniper Switch:

Simply type user name and password; the default username and password for JunOS are **root** with no password.

Login: root

Password: Juniper (this is required for this lab but not on a real juniper switch)

NB: Wait for 20mins before you start to configure

2. Configure Vlan20 on Juniper and name it Accounts, VLAN 30 on Cisco switches and name it Marketing

Configuration Guide Vlans on Juniper

root@Juniper_DataSwitch> edit

Entering configuration mode

{master:0}[edit]

root@Switch_1 # edit vlans

{master:0}[edit vlans]

root@ Juniper_DataSwitch # set Accounts vlan-id 20

root@ Juniper_DataSwitch # commit

configuration check succeeds

commit complete

Exiting configuration mode

{master:0}

root@ Juniper_DataSwitch #show

Accounts {

   vlan-id 20;

}

default {

   vlan-id 1;

root@ Juniper_DataSwitch # run show vlans

Routing instance	VLAN name	Tag	Interfaces
default-switch	Accounts	20	
default-switch	default	1	

3. Configure Trunk Port on the switch connected to the
   Router and describe the port

Configuration Guide for Trunk Port on Juniper

{master:0}[edit]

root@ Juniper_DataSwitch # edit interfaces

root@ Juniper_DataSwitch # edit xe-0/0/0 unit 0 family ethernet-switching

 root@ Juniper_DataSwitch # set interface-mode trunk

root@ Juniper_DataSwitch # set vlan members Accounts

root@ Juniper_DataSwitch # run show configuration | display set | match xe-0/0/0 set interfaces xe-0/0/0 unit 0 family inet dhcp vendor-id Juniper-qfx10002-72q

set interfaces xe-0/0/0:0 unit 0 family inet dhcp vendor-id Juniper-qfx5100-48s-6q

NB: Remove interfaces xe-0/0/0 unit 0 family inet

root@vqfx-re# top

{master:0}[edit]

root@ Juniper_DataSwitch # delete interfaces xe-0/0/0 unit 0 family inet

root@ Juniper_DataSwitch # commit and-quit

configuration check succeeds

commit complete

root@ Juniper_DataSwitch # run show configuration | display set | match xe-0/0/0

set interfaces xe-0/0/0 unit 0 family ethernet-switching interface-mode trunk

set interfaces xe-0/0/0 unit 0 family ethernet-switching vlan members Accounts

set interfaces xe-0/0/0:0 unit 0 family inet dhcp vendor-id Juniper-qfx5100-48s-6q

set interfaces xe-0/0/0:1 unit 0 family inet dhcp vendor-id Juniper-qfx5100-48s-6q

set interfaces xe-0/0/0:2 unit 0 family inet dhcp vendor-id Juniper-qfx5100-48s-6q

{master:0}[edit]

root@ Juniper_DataSwitch # run show interfaces xe-0/0/0

Physical interface: xe-0/0/0, Enabled, Physical link is Up

Interface index: 650, SNMP ifIndex: 519

Link-level type: Ethernet, MTU: 1514, LAN-PHY mode, Speed: 10Gbps,

ogical interface xe-0/0/0.0 (Index 568) (SNMP ifIndex 521)

   Protocol eth-switch, MTU: 1514

   Ping   Flags: Is-Primary, Trunk-Mode

   4. Configure your Access port on the Juniper_Switch
Configuration Guide Access port on Juniper

root@ Juniper_DataSwitch # edit interfaces

              #edit ge-0/0/1 unit 0 family ethernet-switching

              # set interface-mode access

              # set vlan members Accounts

      NB: replace pattern Accounts with desktop (to change the vlan on the interface

root@ Juniper_DataSwitch # run show vlans

Routing instance	VLAN name	Tag	Interfaces
default-switch	Accounts	20	
			xe-0/0/0.0*
			xe-0/0/1.0*
			xe-0/0/2.0*
default-switch	default	1	

5. Configure the routed VLAN interface (RVI) or Integrated routing and bridging (IRB) on all the Switches

Configuration Guide for IRB

{master:0}[edit]

root@ Juniper_DataSwitch # set interfaces irb unit 20 family inet address 192.168.1.2/24

{master:0}[edit]

root@ Juniper_DataSwitch # set vlans Accounts l3-interface irb.20

{master:0}

root@ Juniper_DataSwitch > show interfaces irb terse

Interface	Admin	Link	Proto	Local	Remote
irb	up	up			
irb.20	up	up	inet	192.168.1.2/24	

Configuration Guide for RVI

root@ Juniper_DataSwitch # set interfaces vlan unit 20 family inet address 192.168.1.2/24;

6. Configure the default gateway on the switch
root@ Juniper_DataSwitch # set routing-options static route 0.0.0.0/0 next-hop 192.168.1.1

7. Assign your WAN and Configure Static routing
root@Internet_Router# set description "Cisco_router e1/1"

[edit interfaces em1]

root# set unit 0 family inet address 50.50.50.1/24

[edit]

root@Internet_Router# run show interfaces em1 terse

Interface	Admin	Link	Proto	Local	Remote
em1	Up	Up			
em1.0	up	up	Inet		50.50.50.1/24

root@Internet_Router# run ping 50.50.50.2

PING 50.50.50.2 (50.50.50.2): 56 data bytes

64 bytes from 50.50.50.2: icmp_seq=0 ttl=255 time=1.736 ms

64 bytes from 50.50.50.2: icmp_seq=1 ttl=255 time=1.510 ms

64 bytes from 50.50.50.2: icmp_seq=2 ttl=255 time=1.653 ms

edit]

Configuration Guide for Static routing

set routing-options static route 192.168.2.0/24 next-hop 50.50.50.2

[edit]

root# commit

commit complete

root@Internet_Router# run show route

inet.0: 5 destinations, 5 routes (5 active, 0 holddown, 0 hidden)

+ = Active Route, - = Last Active, * = Both

50.50.50.0/24	*[Direct/0] 00:07:56
	> via em1.0
50.50.50.1/32	*[Local/0] 00:07:57
	Local via em1.0
192.168.1.0/24	*[Direct/0] 00:07:57
	> via em2.20
192.168.1.1/32	*[Local/0] 00:07:57

| 192.168.2.0/24 | Local via em2.20
*[Static/5] 00:01:58
> to 50.50.50.2 via em1.0 |

Test your communication on Cisco environment

PC2> ping 192.168.1.3

84 bytes from 192.168.1.3 icmp_seq=1 ttl=64 time=203.895 ms

84 bytes from 192.168.1.3 icmp_seq=2 ttl=64 time=107.399 ms

84 bytes from 192.168.1.3 icmp_seq=3 ttl=64 time=115.306 ms

PC2> ping 192.168.2.3

84 bytes from 192.168.2.3 icmp_seq=1 ttl=64 time=203.895 ms

84 bytes from 192.168.2.3 icmp_seq=2 ttl=64 time=107.399 ms

84 bytes from 192.168.2.3 icmp_seq=3 ttl=64 time=115.306 ms

LAB GUIDE _2 (MIXED ENVIRONMENT WITH OSPF ROUTING)

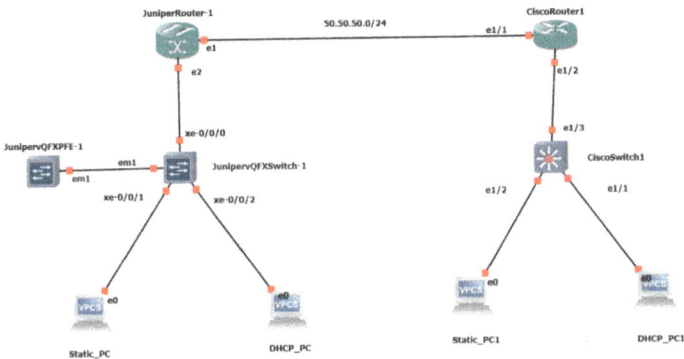

1. Configure all network devices with the following basic information.
2. Assign IP address to the Router and describe the port and the network.
3. Configure the both routers to act as dhcp server
4. Configure Vlan 20 and 30 on the both switches and name it as Accounts and Marketing Respectively
5. Configure Trunk Port on the switch connected to the Router and describe the port
6. Configure your Access port on the Juniper_Switch
7. Configure the routed VLAN interface (RVI) or Integrated routing and bridging (IRB) on all the Switches
8. Assign your WAN and Configure OSPF routing

Configuration guide for OSPF

Instructions:

1. Enter into configuration mode.
2. Enable OSPF routing on the router.
3. Put the interfaces em1 , em2.20 and em2.200 under area 0.

root@Internet_Router# edit protocols ospf

[edit protocols ospf]

root@Internet_Router# edit area 0

[edit protocols ospf area 0.0.0.0]

root@Internet_Router# edit interface em1

[edit protocols ospf area 0.0.0.0 interface em1.0]

root@Internet_Router#exit

[edit protocols ospf area 0.0.0.0]

root@Internet_Router # edit interface em2.20

[edit protocols ospf area 0.0.0.0 interface em2.20]

root@Internet_Router #exit

[edit protocols ospf area 0.0.0.0]

root@Internet_Router # edit interface em2.20

[edit protocols ospf area 0.0.0.0 interface em2.200]

root@Internet_Router # commit
commit complete

root@Internet_Router # run show configuration | display set | match ospf

set protocols ospf area 0.0.0.0 interface em1.0
set protocols ospf area 0.0.0.0 interface em2.20
set protocols ospf area 0.0.0.0 interface em2.200

root@Internet_Router # run show route

inet.0: 6 destinations, 6 routes (6 active, 0 holddown, 0 hidden)

+ = Active Route, - = Last Active, * = Both

50.50.50.0/24	*[Direct/0] 01:50:12
	> via em1.0
50.50.50.1/32	*[Local/0] 01:50:13
	Local via em1.0
192.168.1.0/24	*[Direct/0] 01:50:13
	> via em2.20
192.168.1.1/32	*[Local/0] 01:50:13
	Local via em2.20
192.168.2.0/24	*[OSPF/10] 00:05:38, metric 11
	> to 50.50.50.2 via em1.0
224.0.0.5/32	*[OSPF/10] 00:43:18, metric 1

Cisco_Router1 #show ip route

Codes: L - local, C - connected, S - static, R - RIP, M - mobile, B - BGP

D - EIGRP, EX - EIGRP external, O - OSPF, IA - OSPF inter area

N1 - OSPF NSSA external type 1, N2 - OSPF NSSA external type 2

E1 - OSPF external type 1, E2 - OSPF external type 2

i - IS-IS, su - IS-IS summary, L1 - IS-IS level-1, L2 - IS-IS level-2

ia - IS-IS inter area, * - candidate default, U - per-user static route

o - ODR, P - periodic downloaded static route, H - NHRP, l - LISP

a - application route

+ - replicated route, % - next hop override

Gateway of last resort is not set

50.0.0.0/8 is variably subnetted, 2 subnets, 2 masks

C   50.50.50.0/24 is directly connected, Ethernet1 /1

L   50.50.50.2/32 is directly connected, Ethernet1 /1

O   192.168.1.0/24 [110/11] via 50.50.50.1, 00:03:16, Ethernet1 /1

192.168.2.0/24 is variably subnetted, 2 subnets, 2 masks

C   192.168.2.0/24 is directly connected, Ethernet1 /2

L   192.168.2.1/32 is directly connected, Ethernet1

www.ingramcontent.com/pod-product-compliance
Lightning Source LLC
Chambersburg PA
CBHW040754220326
41597CB00029BA/4773